IN THE LORD'S SERVICE

IN THE LORD'S SERVICE

A GUIDE TO SPIRITUAL DEVELOPMENT

Carlos E. Asay

Deseret Book Company
Salt Lake City, Utah

This book is not an official publication of The Church of Jesus Christ of Latter-day Saints. It has been prepared by the author, and he alone is responsible for the contents.

ISBN 0-87579-390-8

Printed in the United States of America

10   9   8   7   6   5   4   3   2   1

Contents

Contents

Preface

Some time ago, I received a letter from a nephew who was serving as a full-time missionary in the Far East. Near the close of the letter, he wrote: "At this point in my mission I feel a little frustrated. The success isn't coming the way I would like it. It scares me a little. I really love the people here and it sure hurts to see them turn down the gospel. I'm keeping a good attitude about it but if you have any advice that could help, please write."

I was touched by my nephew's words for they conveyed a purity of heart and a sweetness of spirit that is indeed unusual. I responded to Jared's request for help by sending him some material that comprises the major portion of one of the chapters of this book. However, it occurred to me that others might be anxious to receive additional advice about how to fulfill and magnify any calling from the Lord.

So, I began to gather the talks and written messages I have shared with missionaries, mission presidents, priesthood leaders, and others during the past two decades. Some of the messages had been prepared when I served as a full-time mission president; others were presented at the Missionary Training Center in Provo, Utah, or in general conferences of the Church; and, still others were portions of presentations I have given in scores of stake conferences, missionary conferences, mission tours, and seminars for mission presidents and wives. In the end of the gathering process, I had a large collection of information pertaining to Church service.

I have, therefore, included in this book selected advice or counsel that, I pray, may be useful to all the Jareds of the Church—"the pick and flower" of the LDS faith—who are trying to magnify the callings the Lord has given them.

The reader will note that I have cited many, many scriptures in this book. Such scriptures, in company with quotations of Church leaders and my own personal experiences, establish a foundation upon which Church members may build.

It was not my intent to discuss any topic or present information that conflicts with the general instructions of the Church through printed materials or training programs. If there are any inadvertent conflicts or problems with the contents of this book, I assume full and personal responsibility.

Over and over again, as I prepared this text, I was reminded of my own awkwardness of hand and my limited capacity to express myself in writing. My weakness in writing will be made apparent to the reader, for I have stumbled in the placement of my words. However, I assure the reader that I have wished and prayed for the power the brother of Jared possessed—a power that enabled him to write things that were mighty and "overpowering of man to read" (see Ether 12:23–25).

Chapter One

Recognizing the Strength of Your Calling

Most people newly called to positions in The Church of Jesus Christ of Latter-day Saints feel apprehensive about what lies ahead and wonder whether they will be equal to the challenge given them. So, if you have concerns and feelings about a new calling, be assured that these are fairly normal. However, your apprehensions can be turned into strengths if you understand fully the divine nature of your calling and seek to magnify it in the proper way.

Humility versus Pride

Humility is a virtue. One who possesses it is teachable and amenable to instruction. You should, therefore, be humble and "hunger and thirst after righteousness" so that your abilities may be developed, your gifts cultivated, your skills polished, and your confidence increased. In the process, you will "be filled with the Holy Ghost" and strengthened in your calling (3 Nephi 12:6).

At the same time, you must guard against overconfidence and the feeling that you know it all. Such feeling is related to false pride and causes a person to turn a deaf ear to the counsels of God and others (see 2 Nephi 9:28–29).

Usually, when people embark upon a new adventure, such as a calling from the Lord, they are very humble and willing to learn. But, as time goes on and as they gain more and more experience, they may feel "puffed up" in their knowledge and totally self-sufficient. Such was the repeated story in the Book of Mormon, wherein the people went from one extreme to the other—from the holes of humility to the peaks of pride.

You must not permit fear or feelings of inadequacy to inhibit your performance. Similarly, you must never allow yourself to feel that you are beyond reproof or instruction. Seek to be truly humble through the word of God and by recognizing the distinctiveness and the potential strength of your charge or commission.

A Successful Program — Four Reasons

While serving as a mission president in Texas, I had a friend who was a Protestant minister. The man would come occasionally to the mission home and discuss the gospel with me and the missionaries. He was basically a fine man who enjoyed conversing with the members of the office staff.

One day he walked into the office with a troubled look on his face. He was obviously distraught and carrying a heavy burden of some sort. I asked why he was so quiet and glum. He explained that he had just received an appointment from his church to preside over a mission.

I said, "Wonderful! Now you can experience some of the joys I have received through my calling."

"You don't understand," he responded. "I've been a mission president before for my church, and it wasn't a pleasant experience." He then became very pensive and commented: "Your church has the most successful missionary program in the world. Tell me, why do you succeed when so many others fail?"

After I had collected my thoughts, I told him that there were four basic reasons why the Lord's program succeeds. I said, first of all, we succeed because we are led by a living prophet, who is the mouthpiece for God on the earth, who receives inspiration—revelation—on behalf of the Church.

Second, we succeed because we work under the power and authority of the holy priesthood. We don't assume that authority, we don't take it upon ourselves, but it is given to us by the laying on of hands, and we are duly delegated to go out and preach the gospel. We have the priesthood.

Third, I said, we succeed because we are teaching the fulness of the gospel of Jesus Christ as restored in this day. We don't play, as Elder Boyd K. Packer has taught, on one key; we play the entire keyboard. We know where we came from, why we are here in mortality, and where we will go after the death of the body.

And fourth, we succeed because we do what we do on the strength and power of personal testimony. Our young people serve and teach, not because of some promise of remuneration, but rather because they have a testimony. They forego college or delay it and put other personal plans aside so that they can share their testimonies with the world. I said to my friend, "When your church can conduct a program with a prophet directing the work, under the power of the priesthood, with missionaries teaching the fulness of the gospel, and with all involved working on the strength of personal testimonies, you can do exactly what we are doing. And," I added, "there is no need for you to go to all that trouble. We already have the program organized and functioning. Why don't you join us?" He didn't accept my invitation.

The Strengths of Alma's Calling

I didn't realize it at the time, but I was simply sharing with my friend the same reasons Alma cited as the strengths of his calling. The account reads: "Alma went and began to declare the word of God unto the church which was established in the valley of Gideon, according to the revelation of the truth of the word which had been spoken by his fathers, and according to the spirit of prophecy which was in him, according to the testimony of Jesus Christ, the Son of God, who should come to redeem his people from their sins, and the holy order by which he was called" (Alma 6:8).

You will note that Alma fulfilled his calling:

1. "According to the *revelation* of the truth of the word which had been spoken by his fathers." This means that Alma had and used the records or scriptures of his day in doing the work of the Lord.

Such records contained the teachings that had been handed down from father to son—from one generation to another. We today in our callings, like Alma of old, can use the words of our fathers as recorded in the Standard Works of the Church. And, these words of prophets past and present contain a fulness of the gospel that arms us with a weapon more powerful than the sword (see Alma 31:5; 1 Nephi 21:2).

2. "According to the spirit of *prophecy* which was in him." Alma was a prophet and the head of the Church among the Nephites about 83 B.C. He, like the President-Prophet of the Church today, received the necessary inspiration and revelation required to direct the affairs of the Church. Moreover, he had a testimony of Jesus, which is

the spirit of prophecy (see Revelation 19:10). How very blessed are we who serve in the true Church in the twentieth century! Not only are we led by a prophet, but we also enjoy the spirit of revelation or inspiration in magnifying our callings from the Lord.

3. "According to the *testimony* of Jesus Christ, the Son of God, who should come to redeem his people from their sins." Alma himself had a very strong testimony. He knew things that were made known to him "by the Holy Spirit of God." He had fasted and prayed many days to receive this knowledge (see Alma 5:45–47). Therefore, he went forward with confidence and preached fearlessly. And, so it is with those who work in the Church today. They are motivated to serve by what is in their minds and hearts, not by what might be placed in their pocketbooks.

4. "[According to] the *holy order* by which he was called." Alma was called by proper authority, which enabled him to work as an agent of the Lord Jesus Christ. Hence, he spoke as one having authority: he performed mighty miracles, and he saved souls. The servants of God today have also been "called of God, by prophecy, and by the laying on of hands by those who are in authority, to preach the Gospel and administer in the ordinances thereof" (Articles of Faith 1:5). They also perform miracles and receive special endowments of power in full accord with the pattern set by God (see D&C 27:8; Numbers 27:18–23; Mark 3:13–19; Hebrews 5:4).

There are certainly other reasons underlying the success of the work in which we are involved. I don't suppose, however, that many reasons exceed in importance the four discussed above. What is more essential than revelation, prophecy, testimony, and priesthood? Our challenge is fourfold: (1) to know and use effectively the revelations, (2) to follow the prophet and to seek the spirit of prophecy, (3) to

5

nourish and express often your testimony, and (4) to honor the priesthood by which you were called.

Prophecy Fulfilled

In recognizing the strength of your calling, you must also keep in mind the prophecies relating to the great latter-day work. For instance, in 1831 the following revelation was given through Joseph Smith the Prophet: "The keys of the kingdom of God are committed unto man on the earth, and from thence shall the gospel roll forth unto the ends of the earth, as the stone which is cut out of the mountain without hands shall roll forth, until it has filled the whole earth. Wherefore, may the kingdom of God go forth, that the kingdom of heaven may come, that thou, O God, mayest be glorified in heaven so on earth, that thine enemies may be subdued; for thine is the honor, power and glory, forever and ever. Amen." (D&C 65:2, 6.)

For many years the "stone" cut out of the mountain seemed to be at dead rest. Church growth came painfully slow. But, in recent years the growth has accelerated noticeably, and prophecy is being fulfilled. A few statistics illustrate this point rather dramatically.

The Church required 117 years to reach a membership of one million (1830–1947).

It required sixteen years to reach a membership of two million (1947–1963).

It required eight years to reach a membership of three million (1963–1971).

It required seven years to reach a membership of four million (1971–1978).

It required four years to reach a membership of five million (1978–1982).

It required four years to reach a membership of six million (1982–1986).

It required three years to reach a membership of seven million members (1986–1989).

Notice the rapid — even phenomenal — growth since 1963. And, notice how fast the increment of time between each million gained is diminishing. It is altogether conceivable that the Church will be growing at the rate of one million per year before the turn of the century. Of a fact, prophecy is being fulfilled, and the "stone" will, as decreed, fill the whole earth.

At a time when critics were forecasting the demise of the Church and the cloud of persecution hovered over the Saints, the Prophet Joseph Smith boldly proclaimed the standard of truth. Here are his words:

> Persecution has not stopped the progress of truth, but has only added fuel to the flame, it has spread with increasing rapidity, proud of the cause which they have espoused and conscious of their innocence and of the truth of their system amidst calumny and reproach have the elders of this church gone forth, and planted the gospel in almost every state in the Union; it has penetrated our cities, it has spread over our villages, and has caused thousands of our intelligent, noble, and patriotic citizens to obey its divine mandates, and be governed by its sacred truths. It has also spread into England, Ireland, Scotland and Wales: in the year of 1839 where a few of our missionaries were sent over five thousand joined the standard of truth, there are numbers now joining in every land.
>
> Our missionaries are going forth to different nations, and in Germany, Palestine, New Holland, the East Indies, and other places, the standard of truth has been erected: no unhallowed hand can stop the work from progressing, persecutions may rage, mobs may combine, armies may assemble, calumny may defame, but the truth of God will go forth boldly, nobly, and independent, till it has penetrated every continent, visited every clime, swept every

country, and sounded in every ear, till the purposes of God shall be accomplished and the great Jehovah shall say the work is done. ("The Wentworth Letter," *Times and Seasons* 3 [1 March 1842]: 709.)

What a thrilling statement concerning missionary service and the growth of the Church! Only a prophet could see into the future and make such a prediction.

Conclusion

May the Lord bless you in your divine calling. Strive to prepare yourself fully for the challenges that lie ahead. Be humble. Learn quickly. And, remember that "if ye are prepared ye shall not fear" (D&C 38:30). This is the Lord's work; it will not come to naught, and those who oppose it will find themselves fighting against God (see Acts 5:34–40). Yes, the strength of your calling is based upon revelation, prophecy, testimony, priesthood, and more — much more.

Chapter Two

Writing Your
Own Blessing

You undoubtedly received a beautiful blessing when you were set apart in your calling. I encourage you to think often of that blessing throughout the term of your service and to remind yourself periodically of the blessings pronounced in your behalf. You must remember, however, that the blessings mentioned are predicated upon your faithfulness.

A Mission Blessing

A number of years ago, while laboring in the Palestine-Syrian Mission, I was called to serve as the second counselor in the mission presidency. After I was sustained by the members, President Alma Sonne of the European Mission set me apart for the new calling. In doing so, he pronounced a most memorable blessing, one I shall never forget.

At the conclusion of the blessing, I thanked Elder Sonne for the beautiful and inspiring words he had spoken. He graciously accepted my expression of gratitude; however, he placed his hand upon my shoulder, looked intently into my eyes, and said, "Elder Asay, I had the power and right to say what I said, but remember, you will write your own blessing by the way you live and serve." Then he added, "Go and write the best blessing that has ever been written."

We do, in fact, write our own blessings by the way we live and serve. Blessings do not come to us automatically and simply because hands have been placed upon our heads and beautiful words spoken. Blessings flow from the divine source and are channeled to mortals when laws are honored and when lives are made to harmonize with the will of Deity. It is written: "There is a law, irrevocably decreed in heaven before the foundations of this world, upon which all blessings are predicated—and when we obtain any blessing from God, it is by obedience to that law upon which it is predicated" (D&C 130:20–21).

Patriarchal Blessings

When a stake patriarch places his hands upon our heads, gives us a blessing, and inspires us with pronounced prophecies and promises, an exciting beginning has been made. It is left to us to keep those prophecies and promises riveted in our minds—regarding them as attainable goals—and proceed forward with righteous living and faithful service so that we might draw claim upon the related blessings.

By way of illustration, the patriarch stands with us at the starter's gate. He envisions for us the race that lies ahead. With the aid of his special gifts, he outlines the rules of the contest, describes the challenges we will face, and cites the laurels that may be won. However, we, the runners, must stay in the marked lane, abide the rules, cover the course, and cross the finish line if we expect to receive the victor's prize.

Being Set Apart for a Calling

When you were set apart in your calling, you were commissioned to participate in a divine work. You were probably reminded of the importance of such service and instructed in how you should live and conduct your affairs. You may have received such promises as the development of a Christlike character, a forgiveness of sins, and the acquisition of unspeakable joy. Nonetheless, these and other stated blessings do not come by the wave of a wand or the sound of the lips. They come in accord with desire and a worthy performance of duty. The Christlike character grows step by step and blossoms as a result of disciplined and righteous living; the forgiveness of sins occurs as we repent, climb for higher ground, and exert the effort to lift or save others; and, the unspeakable joy comes as we witness one of the miracles of the gospel — the transformation for good of those we faithfully serve.

Temple Sealings

When we are sealed in the temple to a companion for time and eternity, an authorized agent teaches us much concerning celestial marriage. In the process, he extends marvelous blessings pertaining to (1) the prospects of participating in the first resurrection, (2) all the blessings of Abraham, Isaac, and Jacob, and (3) the blessings of powers and kingdoms. But the sealer also calls to our attention that such blessings will be ours only if we are true and faithful to the covenants made in the temple.

The fact that a couple kneels at an altar in the house of the Lord and exchanges sacred vows is no guarantee of abiding happiness here or hereafter. Abiding happiness is claimed through acts of kindness, unselfish living, fidelity, charity, and all else associated with God's form of marriage. One of the early chapters of an enduring union is written as we are sealed in the temple; however, the final chapters with all their blessings are written as we learn, live, and love in holy matrimony.

The Power of Agency

When you are called to serve in any Church capacity, be it a teaching or a presiding assignment, keep in mind the sons of Lehi. All of them—Laman, Lemuel, Sam, Nephi, Jacob, and Joseph—were extended blessings. All of them, I suspect, felt the weight of their father's hands upon their heads. Their ears received the sounds from his voice as blessings were spoken. Still, they were left with their agency—the right to choose good or evil, the right to pen or erase their own blessings. Lehi warned his eldest sons: "If ye will hearken unto him [Nephi] I leave unto you a blessing, yea, even my first blessing. But if ye will not hearken unto him I take away my first blessing, yea, even my blessing, and it shall rest upon him" (2 Nephi 1:28–29).

Despite the warning, the eldest sons rejected the Spirit of God because their hearts were hard and their minds were blinded to the truth. They lost their privileges and were cursed. The other sons heeded their father's counsel, followed a path of righteousness, and retained the greater privileges.

These things cause me to reflect upon the teachings of the prophet Alma. He spoke of faith, callings, ordinations, and good works. He referred to those who had been called and prepared for holy callings. Among other truths, he declared, "They have been called to this holy calling on account of their faith, while others would reject the Spirit of God on account of the hardness of their hearts and blindness of their minds, while, if it had not been for this they might have had as great privilege as their brethren" (Alma 13:4).

Hardness of heart and blindness of mind not only cause

12

many to forfeit service opportunities but also deprive some people of the privileges and blessings associated with honorable service. John Greenleaf Whittier must have had this in mind when he wrote, "Of all sad words of tongue or pen, the saddest are these: 'It might have been.' "

Father's Blessings

Soon after my eighteenth birthday, I felt the weight of my father's hands upon my head as he gave me a special blessing. This was occasioned by my entrance into the military during World War II. My father anticipated my apprehensions about leaving home and becoming involved in the business of fighting. So in the blessing he gave me reassurance. He also admonished me to rely upon the Lord and to keep the commandments. Specifically, he told me to live the Word of Wisdom (avoid the use of tobacco and alcohol) and to maintain the moral standards of the Church. Then he promised me that if I would do all of these things, I would return home safe, whole, and unstained by the world.

Throughout my stint in the army, the words of my father remained vivid in my mind and heart. Many times I was enticed to live less than the Latter-day Saint kind of life. But, each time temptation presented itself, the promise of returning home safe and well resounded in my ears. I wanted to draw claim upon the blessings cited by my father. In due time the pronounced blessings and more were mine; I had written my own blessing; I had proven the words: "Behold, this is the promise of the Father unto you if you continue faithful" (D&C 108:5).

Worthy of a Father's Love

I once interviewed a very humble young man who was just beginning his mission. We had not exchanged many words when he began to sob almost uncontrollably. I wondered what was wrong.

After many tears had dropped upon the carpet, he looked up at me and said: "President, it isn't what you are thinking. I am not guilty of any major sin. But rather, it is all the little errors which I have made over the years that come flooding back to my mind, making me wonder whether I am worthy to serve the Lord."

I put my arm around the missionary and assured him that his call was inspired, for he possessed a broken heart and a contrite spirit and had met all of the expected qualifications. I indicated that the path of youth was generally very slippery and that few escape slips and slides along the way. I also read to him the following promise: "Brethren, if any of you do err from the truth, and one convert him; let him know, that he which converteth the sinner from the error of his way shall save a soul from death, and shall hide a multitude of sins" (James 5:19–20).

He responded to my words and the scripture by saying, "That's what I want more than anything else." Then he added, "Tell me, president, what must I do to claim the promise and to be forgiven of my foolish transgressions?"

I advised him to be completely honest, obedient, and faithful in fulfilling his holy calling. And, so he was. During the next two years, the only complaint I ever heard from the young man's companions was, "He is working me to death."

The time passed quickly, and the young man's mission came to an end. When he reported at the mission office for his closing interview and testimonial, he was a spiritual giant — one who had been sanctified through his selfless service.

As the missionary bore his final testimony in the mission field, he became very emotional. Among other inspiring things, he stated: "Few of you know that my father is a patriarch and a very demonstrative man. He is filled with love and is quick to hug and kiss others."

The elder paused, wiped away a tear, and continued: "Before my mission, I tried to avoid my father. Whenever he attempted to embrace me, I would shrink away and push his arms aside. I did so because I felt unworthy of his love."

A longer pause followed with still more tears. Then the young man cried: "I can't wait to get home tonight; I can't wait to feel my father's arms about me. For the first time in many years, I feel worthy of his love!"

All of us are much like my missionary associate. We, too, seek the love and approbation of our fathers, both mortal and heavenly. Such love and approbation, however, will come only if we live and serve properly and remain faithful to the end.

Conclusion

Over the years Elder Sonne's words, "You will write your own blessing by the way you live and serve," have echoed again and again in my mind.

Each time I have been called to serve in a Church position, each time I have received a setting-apart blessing, I have reflected back to the sage counsel I received in the mission field. And, I have consciously striven to live and serve in such a manner that I might draw claim upon all the blessings found through the gospel of Jesus Christ and in the kingdom of God on earth.

Said the Lord, "All who will have a blessing at my hands [or the hands of priesthood leaders] shall abide the law which was appointed for that blessing, and the conditions thereof, as were instituted from before the foundation of the world" (D&C 132:5).

As Elder Sonne challenged me, so I challenge you to abide the laws, expectations, and conditions linked to your calling and to go and write the best setting-apart blessing that has ever been written.

Chapter Three

Obtaining and Building
a Personal Testimony

Perhaps when you were called to your position, you bore your testimony, acknowledging your weaknesses and pledging to serve the Lord with a singleness of purpose. Your testimony of the Savior and his work is an important tool in fulfilling your calling.

What Is a Testimony?

Elder Bruce R. McConkie has written:

> A testimony of the gospel is the sure knowledge, received by revelation from the Holy Ghost, of the divinity of the great latter-day work. . . . Three great truths must be included in every valid testimony:
> 1. That Jesus Christ is the Son of God and the Savior of the world (D&C 46:13);
> 2. That Joseph Smith is the Prophet of God through whom the gospel was restored in this dispensation; and,
> 3. That The Church of Jesus Christ of Latter-day Saints

is "the only true and living church upon the face of the whole earth" (D&C 1:30). (*Mormon Doctrine,* 2nd ed. [Salt Lake City: Bookcraft, 1966], pp. 785–86.)

Each of the Standard Works of the Church is a testimony in and of itself, for all testify of the truths mentioned above. Each is a witness or testament of God and his divine purposes. Each is a library of testimonies born by prophets and apostles who received the testimony of Jesus and enjoyed the spirit of prophecy (see Revelation 19:10).

From the Old Testament, we draw such inspiring declarations as Job's: "Oh that my words were now written! oh that they were printed in a book! That they were graven with an iron pen and lead in the rock for ever! For I know that my redeemer liveth, and that he shall stand at the latter day upon the earth: And though after my skin worms destroy this body, yet in my flesh shall I see God" (Job 19:23–26).

From the New Testament, we receive this stirring witness of Peter's: "Lord, to whom shall we go? thou hast the words of eternal life. And we believe and are sure that thou art that Christ, the Son of the Living God" (John 6:68–69).

From the Book of Mormon, we hear the bold testimony of Abinadi: "There is a resurrection, therefore the grave hath no victory, and the sting of death is swallowed up in Christ. He is the light and the life of the world; yea, a light that is endless, that can never be darkened. . . . Repent of your sins, and remember that only in and through Christ ye can be saved" (Mosiah 16:8–9, 13).

From the Doctrine and Covenants, we read the thrilling vision given Joseph Smith and Sidney Rigdon: "And now, after the many testimonies which have been given of him, this is the testimony, last of all, which we give of him: That he lives! For we saw him, even on the right hand of God; and we heard the voice bearing record that he is the Only

Begotten of the Father—that by him, and through him, and of him, the worlds are and were created, and the inhabitants thereof are begotten sons and daughters unto God" (D&C 76:22–24).

Yes, so long as we have the holy scriptures we are "compassed about with so great a cloud of witnesses" (Hebrews 12:1). And, "in the mouth of as many witnesses as seemeth him good will he establish his word; and wo be unto him that rejecteth the word of God!" (2 Nephi 27:14).

How Is a Testimony Recognized?

While serving as a bishop, I invited a faithful and clean young man to serve a mission. He refused. I was shocked; I had not anticipated his answer. He claimed that he did not have a testimony, and he felt that it would be hypocritical of him to serve without a testimony. Six months later I called him in and issued the invitation once more. Again he said no, adding that he still didn't have a testimony. This time the Spirit came to my rescue. I said, "Young man, answer me some basic questions. Is there a God in heaven?"

"Well, of course there is. If I didn't believe there was a God, I wouldn't pray."

I said, "Thank you. Is Jesus the Christ?"

"Yes, of course he is. I've never doubted that fact. He is the Son of God; he is my Savior."

I said, "Thank you. Was Joseph Smith the Prophet of the Restoration?"

"Oh certainly, Bishop," he said. "I feel certain that he received a divine commission from God to perform his work."

I said, "Thank you. One more question, young man. Is the man whom we sustain as the president of the Church really a prophet?"

A big smile crossed his face, and he asked, "When do I

leave?" He had the testimony all the time. He just had not realized what a testimony was and how to verbalize it.

Some young people grow up in the Church and take many things for granted, including a testimony. They are exposed to saving truths but ask few integrating questions. They hear a string of testimonies but never bear their own. They see the gospel work miracles in the lives of people yet never make the connection between principle and practice. Hence, the raw ingredients of a testimony are all about them, only awaiting the mixing and stirring actions required in the formation of a testimony.

How Is a Testimony Obtained?

A short time ago, two missionaries found and taught a woman who was interested in receiving the fulness of the gospel. The missionaries taught her all of the discussions; she attended Church meetings and made other commitments. However, she refused the invitation to be baptized, saying that she had not received a personal witness or testimony of the restored gospel.

One day this nonmember woman went to a physician's office for a physical examination. Upon her arrival at the office, the waiting room was full of patients. Therefore, while waiting for her appointment, she took from her purse a copy of the Book of Mormon and began to read it.

A man who was sitting across the room watched with deep interest as she read the book. When his curiosity got the better of him, he crossed the room and sat down beside her. He asked, "What are you reading?"

"The Book of Mormon," she responded.

"What is that?" he said. "I've never heard of the Book of Mormon."

The woman proceeded to tell him what the missionaries had told her. She spoke about Joseph Smith, the coming forth of the Book of Mormon, and the account of the ancients of America. In the process, she marveled at how much she had remembered from the teachings of the missionaries.

At the end of the woman's explanation, the man said, "Very, very interesting — that's the most intriguing story I've ever heard. But," he added, "I have one question. Is the book true?"

The Spirit enveloped the young woman, and almost instinctively she declared with excitement and strong emotion, "Yes, yes, it is true!" Tears came to her eyes as she realized that her testimony was born as it was borne. She rushed home following the doctor's appointment, called the missionaries, and requested baptism.

The experience of this young woman verifies a principle taught by Elder Boyd K. Packer. He stated:

> A testimony is to be *found* in the *bearing* of it! Somewhere in your quest for spiritual knowledge, there is that "leap of faith," as the philosophers call it. It is the moment when you have gone to the edge of the light and stepped into the darkness to discover that the way is lighted ahead for just a footstep or two. "The spirit of man," as the scripture says, indeed "is the candle of the Lord" (Prov. 20:27).
>
> It is one thing to receive a witness from what you have read or what another has said; and that is a necessary beginning. It is quite another to have the Spirit confirm to you in your bosom that what *you* have testified is true. Can you not see that it will be supplied as you share it? As you give that which you have, there is a replacement, with increase! ("The Candle of the Lord," *Ensign*, January 1983, pp. 54–55.)

Elder Packer's words and the experience of the young woman are in harmony with the teachings of the Christ. The Savior taught: "My doctrine is not mine, but his that sent me. If any man will do his will, he shall know of the doctrine, whether it be of God, or whether I speak of myself" (John 7:16–17).

This statement reminds us that we gain a testimony of tithing by paying it; we gain a testimony of the Word of Wisdom by living it; we gain a testimony of the Book of Mormon by reading and praying about it; we gain a testimony of living prophets by following their counsel; and, we obtain and retain a testimony of the gospel by sharing it with others. It is in the doing or application of something that its truthfulness is tested.

One of the finest summary statements of how a testimony is obtained was expressed by Alma. He said:

> I testify unto you that I do know that these things whereof I have spoken are true. And how do ye suppose that I know of their surety? Behold, I say unto you they are made known unto me by the Holy Spirit of God. Behold, I have fasted and prayed many days that I might know these things of myself. And now I do know of myself that they are true; for the Lord God hath made them manifest unto me by his Holy Spirit; and this is the spirit of revelation which is in me.
>
> And moreover, I say unto you that it has thus been revealed unto me, that the words which have been spoken by our fathers are true, even so according to the spirit of prophecy which is in me, which is also by the manifestation of the Spirit of God (Alma 5:45–47).

What Is Pure Testimony?

Reference to "pure testimony" was made by the prophet Alma, who forsook the judgment seat to reclaim an apostate people. It is recorded that he could see "no way that he might reclaim [the people] save it were in bearing down in pure testimony against them" (Alma 4:19).

One wonders what it is that makes testimony pure. Is

it the message? the testator? the means or method used? Or, is it a combination of all of these? Alma stated that he would use "the word of God" to stir them up in remembrance of their duty and to pull down their pride, craftiness, and contentions. So, it seems to me that the pure "doctrine of Christ, and the only and true doctrine of the Father" is requisite (2 Nephi 31:21). Moreover, it seems to me that the testator must be one "with a pure heart and clean hands" and one who is filled with charity or the pure love of Christ (see Alma 5:19; Moroni 7:47). A pure doctrine taught by a pure man or woman with pure motive will result in a pure testimony.

Testimonies and the Book of Mormon

A discussion of testimony would be incomplete without reference to the Book of Mormon and the Prophet Joseph Smith. I say this because both the book and the man played vital and companion roles in the restoration of the gospel. And, if the book is true, then the translator was a prophet; contrariwise, if the man was a prophet, then the book he translated was of divine origin and fulfilled divine purposes.

Recently, a research group published a statement about the Book of Mormon and its translator that merits thoughtful consideration:

> Consider these amazing facts about the Book of Mormon and the astonishingly short time Joseph took to translate it:
>
> Recent research into the historical record shows it unlikely that any more than 65 to 75 days were involved in the actual translation. . . . These were busy days. From April to June, one must also allow Joseph time to reveal several sections of the D&C; to restore the Priesthood; to baptize others; to give personal instructions to Oliver, Hyrum and Samuel Smith, and Joseph Knight; to move

on buckboard from Harmony to Fayette (3 to 4 days); to obtain the copyright; and to eat and sleep.

In practical terms alone, this is an impressive feat: 7 to 10 current book pages per day, final copy, day after day. Imagine, on average, only a day and a half to compose King Benjamin's speech, or a week to do 1 Nephi, or a couple of hours for Alma 36! No wonder Oliver wrote in 1834, *"These were days never to be forgotten."* (*Insights: An Ancient Window* [Provo, Utah: Foundation for Ancient Research and Mormon Studies], February 1986, p. 1.)

The work of Joseph Smith is even more amazing when we compare the compilation of the King James Version of the Bible and the translation of the Book of Mormon. Consider these additional facts:

The Bible was translated by six companies of scholars consisting of fifty-four members. The Book of Mormon was translated by one relatively unlearned farm boy.

The translation of the Bible required four years of labor (from 1607 to 1611). The translation of the Book of Mormon required from sixty-five to seventy-five days (April to June, 1829).

The average production rate for the Bible was one page per day. The average production rate for the Book of Mormon was seven to ten pages per day—final copy. (See Bible Dictionary, p. 625.)

No one, however learned and skilled, could have, without divine assistance, done what Joseph Smith did in bringing forth the Book of Mormon. But, with the help of the Lord, Joseph Smith produced a work rightfully referred to as a marvelous work and a wonder. Each page shouts aloud, "This is a book of divine origin!" Of a surety, the Book of Mormon is not a man-made publication. It is another witness of Christ and his prophet, even the Prophet Joseph Smith.

The Promise of Testimony in the Book of Mormon

A further testimony of the Book of Mormon is the promise given the reader in the closing chapter. Moroni, the prophet who sealed up the record about A.D. 421, wrote:

> Behold, I would exhort you that when ye shall read these things, if it be wisdom in God that ye should read them, that ye would remember how merciful the Lord hath been unto the children of men, from the creation of Adam even down until the time that ye shall receive these things, and ponder it in your hearts.
>
> And when ye shall receive these things, I would exhort you that ye would ask God, the Eternal Father, in the name of Christ, if these things are not true; and if ye shall ask with a sincere heart, with real intent, having faith in Christ, he will manifest the truth of it unto you, by the power of the Holy Ghost.
>
> And by the power of the Holy Ghost ye may know the truth of all things. (Moroni 10:3–5.)

Please observe that a testimony of the book is centered in the power of the Holy Ghost—the sure witness of truth—and that four essential actions are requisite:

1. *Read.* Read the book with righteous intent and with an eye of faith.

2. *Remember.* Remember the mercy of the Lord as revealed in the plan of salvation, the love of the Lord as demonstrated in the Atonement, and the concern of the Lord as shown in his watch care over mankind since the creation of the earth.

3. *Ponder.* Ponder in your heart the things you read. Allow the thoughts of the mind to mesh with the feelings of your heart so that the "inner man" becomes actively involved in the quest for truth.

4. *Ask.* Ask God, in the name of Christ, if the things

you read are not true. Do this with a sincere heart, with real intent or a pureness of motive, and with faith in Christ.

If you take these steps, your prayers will be answered and the promise will be realized. God does not lie, and, if he says that he will manifest the truth to you or any person, he will do so through the power of the Holy Ghost.

Conclusion

I have read the Book of Mormon many times and received in each reading a confirmation of the truthfulness of the book and its translator. It is the word of God, and through it we can testify that we have heard the Lord's voice and know of his words (see D&C 18:34–36).

May we have the faith to do and to share goodness with others, as did the widow of Zarephath. By so doing, our barrel of faith shall not waste nor will our cruse of testimony fail (see 1 Kings 17:8–16).

Chapter Four

Courting the Spirit of Your Calling

Whenever I visit the Missionary Training Center at Provo, Utah, I feel a strong spirit of missionary service. It is an exhilarating and wonderful feeling that seems to surround those who are sincerely invested in proclaiming the gospel and saving souls.

Since much of your success depends upon your determination to court the spirit of your calling, I desire to share some thoughts I pray will help you understand it better.

One Wish

While I was serving as a mission president, my wife and I were privileged to attend a training seminar in Nauvoo. The instructions we received from the General Authorities and others in that three-day conference were most inspiring. A testimony meeting was held as the concluding session of the seminar. Many strong testimonies were shared, including a memorable expression of faith by President Hugh B.

Brown. As President Brown finished his message, he closed his eyes and in the attitude of prayer said, "If God would grant me but one wish, it would be that all missionaries in the world would *obtain* and *retain* the spirit of their callings."

President Brown's one wish was not voiced in a casual or flippant manner. He expressed a desire that flowed from the innermost part of his heart. His mind was not fixed upon personal wealth or convenience; he was preoccupied with thoughts of missionary service and the extension of that service worldwide. He knew that the work of God would spread among all nations and peoples only as fast as the missionary spirit was reflected by those called to declare repentance.

A Double Portion of Spirit

Whenever I think of the Nauvoo experience with President Brown, I'm reminded of the biblical incident involving two Old Testament prophets. Elijah, as you will recall, had been a faithful and powerful servant of the Lord. As his ministry on earth drew to an end, he met with Elisha and stated, "Ask what I shall do for thee, before I be taken away from thee." Elisha, I suspect, could have requested endowments of gold, fame, or other things of a worldly nature. However, he replied, "I pray thee, let a double portion of thy spirit be upon me" (2 Kings 2:9).

Elijah may have been surprised by Elisha's wish, for he answered, "Thou hast asked a hard thing: nevertheless, if thou see me when I am taken from thee, it shall be so unto thee; but if not, it shall not be so" (2 Kings 2:10).

A chariot and horses of fire did appear, and Elijah went up in a whirlwind into heaven. Elisha saw it all! The record indicates that the mantle of Elijah fell upon his successor,

Elisha, and those who saw him testified, "The spirit of Elijah doth rest on Elisha" (see 2 Kings 2:11–15).

It seems appropriate for me to ask what spirit rests upon you? Do you have the spirit of your calling? Do you know what it is? Do you know how it is obtained? Retained?

What Is the Spirit of a Calling?

A definition or description of the spirit of one's calling, as such, is not found in holy writ. However, some understanding of that spirit is obtained by examining a kindred spirit—the spirit of Elijah. According to what is recorded in the Doctrine and Covenants, the spirit of Elijah is a power or influence that, if planted in the soul, turns our hearts to our fathers and the promises made to the fathers (see D&C 2:2).

Elder Boyd K. Packer adds this enlightening explanation: "The spirit of Elijah spoken of by the Prophet [Joseph Smith] . . . is something very real. When a member of the Church comes under its influence, it is a powerful, compelling force which motivates him with a desire to be attending to genealogical and temple work. It leaves him anxious over the well-being of his forebears. When that spirit comes, somehow we desire to know more about those forebears— we desire to *know* them" (*The Holy Temple* [Salt Lake City: Bookcraft, 1980], p. 210).

Please note that the spirit of Elijah is referred to as "a powerful, compelling force." It creates desire; it turns one's heart and thoughts outward and toward others; it causes concern for the well-being of others; and it motivates saving actions.

The spirit of a calling is similar to the spirit of Elijah. Its effect upon people is seen in the following scriptural accounts:

Enos—Desire for the welfare of others. Enos's soul was

starved, so he turned to God in prayer. In response to his petitions heavenward, his sins were forgiven and his faith in Christ strengthened. Immediately thereafter, a desire — a new desire — sprouted from deep within his heart. "I began to feel a desire," he said, "for the welfare of my brethren, the Nephites; wherefore, I did pour out my whole soul unto God for them" (Enos 1:9). He also voiced these same desires and prayers in behalf of his brethren and his enemies, the Lamanites.

The Sons of Mosiah — Desire to proclaim the gospel. The sons of Mosiah, as you will recall, rebelled against their father and all righteousness. In fact, at the height of their rebellion, they sought actively to destroy the Church and to lead people astray. However, after they had received a spiritual, converting experience, they repented of their sins and zealously worked to repair all the injuries they had done to the Church. A change came over them; their hearts softened and turned; and they became "desirous that salvation should be declared to every creature, for they could not bear that any human soul should perish" (Mosiah 28:3).

Abish — Opportunity to build belief and faith. The Book of Mormon describes Abish as one who had been "converted unto the Lord for many years, on account of a remarkable vision of her father" (Alma 19:16). At a critical moment, she responded to a prompting within, "supposing that this opportunity . . . would cause [her people] to believe in the power of God, therefore she ran forth from house to house, making it known unto the people" (Alma 19:17).

Alma — Desire to preach with angelic power. Alma, one of the great Nephite prophets, developed a love for God and his work that caused him to cry: "O that I were an angel, and could have the wish of mine heart, that I might go forth and speak with the trump of God, with a voice to shake the earth, and cry repentance unto every people!" (Alma 29:1).

Alma stated further: "This is my glory, that perhaps I may be an instrument in the hands of God to bring some soul to repentance; and this is my joy" (Alma 29:9). Later, when Alma had observed the wickedness, perverseness, and false worship of a people, he begged of God: "Behold, O Lord, their souls are precious, and many of them are our brethren; therefore, give unto us, O Lord, power and wisdom that we may bring these, our brethren, again unto thee" (Alma 31:35).

Paul—Willing to impart his own soul to others. The Apostle Paul, one of the greatest of all missionaries, had much to say about true ministers of the gospel. He told of how he and others had declared the word in Philippi. Among other things, he said, "Being affectionately desirous of you, we were willing to have imparted unto you, not the gospel of God only, but also our own souls, because ye were dear unto us" (1 Thessalonians 2:8).

Many other scriptures could be cited to illustrate the spirit that prompts men and women to righteous service in the Church of Jesus Christ. Paul spoke of affectionate desire and a willingness to give all (1 Thessalonians 2:8); Alma recognized the worth of souls and a desire to cry repentance (Alma 29:1, 9); Abish was an opportunist and wanted others to believe in God (Alma 19:16–17); the sons of Mosiah did not want to lose one precious human soul (Mosiah 28:3); and Enos cradled a desire for the welfare of his brethren (Enos 1:9). These scriptural accounts and others testify of a spirit—real, powerful, and compelling—that leads us to reach outward in preaching, teaching, and service. Such influences, combined as one, might be referred to as the spirit of one's calling.

The Breath of Life

Let us consider the spirit of missionary work. Just as the spirit, or "breath of life," animates the human body, so does the missionary spirit give life and vitality to the missionary. Without that spirit, a missionary drags through his day; time weighs heavy on his hands; he is listless; nothing seems urgent; and his every effort is labored. However, with that spirit—even the spirit of his calling—the missionary assumes lively and assertive qualities. He immerses himself in his work and moves forward with zeal and full investment of energies.

An unseen breeze will animate the leaves on a tree. A silent shadow will stir into action the sleeping deer. The unseen and silent missionary spirit animates and stirs into action those called to proclaim the gospel of Jesus Christ.

Have you ever played on a team that had no spirit, no desire to win? If you have, I think that you will agree that such a team was always a pushover. Have you ever competed against someone who played without spirit? To such a person every bad break is a major calamity, every point scored against him too much to overcome, and every decision of the referee a colossal error. On the other hand, the team or individual with spirit is always a formidable opponent. Spirit has a way of compensating for many things. It causes the adrenalin and creative juices to flow. It infuses a will to keep trying against almost insurmountable odds. And, it provides that winning edge that inevitably leads to success.

Though the missionary spirit is without measurable height or weight, its presence or absence is clearly evident. For example, the spirit is absent when missionaries:

• Speak negatively about the people with whom they are working.

• Permit one rejection (at the door or otherwise) to ruin their day.

• Offer prayers that are rushed, general in nature, and without feeling.

• Approach half-heartedly the study of the scriptures.

• Are reluctant to challenge investigators to live the gospel or submit to baptism.

• Take no pride in the way they teach the discussions.

• Find it difficult in the morning to rise and start the day.

• Are without a smile and cheerful disposition.

• Hesitate to bear testimony or follow a promising lead.

All of these symptoms are related to a sagging or dead missionary spirit. One symptom feeds upon another, and all should be avoided like the plague.

The missionary spirit is obviously present when missionaries:

• Have a spring in their walk.

• See possibilities for success all about them.

• Demonstrate love for the gospel and a love for people.

• Express in their countenances the light of the gospel as they bear witness of the truth.

• Take advantage of every contacting and teaching opportunity.

• Scramble for leads and sense an urgency in their work.

• Do all they can and more and leave the rest to the Lord.

• See goodness and possibilities in everyone.

• Write frequently in their journals about spiritual experiences.

• Feel as Ether felt. He "could not be restrained because of the Spirit of the Lord which was in him. . . . He did cry from the morning, even until the going down of the sun, exhorting the people to believe in God unto repentance" (Ether 12:2–3).

Please note that all of these evidences of the missionary spirit are positive in nature and reflect faith in God and one's calling. Many of these evidences could be seen in any other Church calling as well.

33

A Marvelous Phenomenon

A marvelous phenomenon occurs among people when the light of the gospel illuminates their lives. Almost instinctively, it seems, that light of truth sparks a desire to share. When our minds are expanded by new knowledge, we want others to know; when our spirits are elevated by heavenly influence, we want others to feel; and when our lives are filled with goodness, we want others, particularly those we love, to enjoy similar experiences.

You will recall that in a dream, Lehi "beheld a tree, whose fruit was desirable to make one happy." So he went forth, partook of the fruit, and was filled with joy. Then, according to the record, he "began to be desirous that [his] family should partake of it also; for," he said, "I knew that it was desirable above all other fruit." This fruit motivated Lehi to beckon to his family and "with a loud voice" invite them to come to him and partake (see 1 Nephi 8:10–12, 15).

Not long ago, I heard the testimony of a new convert — a young man obviously touched by the Spirit. He said that it was his great desire to share the restored gospel with his family and friends. With tears in his eyes and a quiver in his voice, he stated, "I want them to know what I know. I want them to feel what I feel. I want them to do what I have done."

Courting the Spirit of Your Calling

You may have expected the spirit of your calling to fall upon you like a blanket at the time you were set apart. If this was the case, you may have been disappointed. Such a spirit must be sought and courted in a very special manner.

I should like to suggest five courting actions that, if taken, will attract that special spirit and cause it to hover over you and your work.

1. *Remember God's goodness.* Enos remembered the

teachings of his father. This exercise in recall influenced him to repent and to obtain a forgiveness of sins. It also directed his thoughts toward his brethren, particularly those who knew not God. Recalling Christ's mercy, teachings, and work will naturally promote the desire to share the blessings of full salvation. Souls become precious when we remember their beginnings. Reaching out to others becomes important when we remember how God has reached out to us.

2. *Cultivate a desire or will.* Alma taught that God grants "unto men according to their desire" or wills (Alma 29:4). We must, therefore, cultivate a desire or build a will to serve before we can hope to obtain the spirit of our calling. Even though we are called to serve, God will not offend our agency by imposing or thrusting an unwanted influence. So we must want that spirit and actively seek it.

3. *Study and search the scriptures.* Once the will is in place, we must study and prepare for the work. It would be foolish to expect the spirit of a calling to fall upon or abide with someone who does not understand the basics of the gospel. It is a knowledge of Christ's atonement that prompts a father to declare repentance to his children. It is an understanding of baptism that causes a missionary to press for baptism. It is the view of eternal life that helps a teacher understand the true value of a soul.

4. *Engage in humble and sincere prayer.* Prayer, in company with study, is essential to obtaining the spirit of one's calling. Having sought by study, we must seek the spirit of our calling next by prayer. The earnest and sincere prayer will confirm what we have studied. Moreover, it will stir feelings and cleanse the mind so that a singleness of purpose will find place. The sincere prayer would properly include the request for the Spirit of the Lord, which is really the source of the spirit of one's calling, with all its blessings and powers.

35

5. *Work, work, and work.* President Ezra Taft Benson has said on many occasions that the most important aspect of our work is the Spirit. And, he has instructed that there are three ways to obtain the Spirit in our callings. One is work, two is work, and three is work. We learn to read by reading; we learn to walk by walking; and we catch the spirit of our work by working. You have heard the ad, "Try it— you'll like it." In reference to the spirit of Church service, we might say, "Try it and you will get it."

These courting actions remind me of an experience I had with a young missionary several years ago. The young man had lost the spirit of his calling and wanted to go home. I pleaded with him to try once more and to work diligently that he might regain the proper enthusiasm for the work. Reluctantly, he accepted a new companion, a zone leader, and promised to give it one more chance.

A week or so later, I received a telephone call from a stranger. He asked, "Are you in charge of the Mormon missionaries in the Dallas area?"

"Yes," I responded, "I am the mission president."

"Well," he said, "I regret to inform you that two of your missionaries were involved in a head-on automobile collision at an intersection near my place of business, and I think that both are dead."

I quickly took down an address, summoned one of my assistants, and sped to the place of the accident. Upon arrival at the scene, I saw two demolished cars, a large crowd of people, and broken glass all over the street. I pushed my way through the crowd, trying to find someone who could tell me the conditions and whereabouts of my missionaries.

Suddenly my assistant shouted, "Come here, President, I've found one of them." I rushed to his side, and there was the zone leader. Though he was on his feet, he was as white as a sheet and in a state of shock.

"Where's your companion?" I asked.

"Oh, they took him away in the ambulance—he was bleeding badly."

I said, "Elder, they should have taken you too. You need medical attention."

My assistant and I helped the injured zone leader into the car and sped to the hospital.

Upon arrival at the emergency room, I sought help for the missionary and inquired about his companion. A nurse told me to follow her. We reached a waiting room, she drew a curtain aside, and I saw my missionary. He was covered with more blood than bandages, and my heart nearly stopped beating.

Suddenly the missionary rose up in bed and bellowed: "Come in, President, we've had a wonderful day! Before that drunk smacked us with his car, we placed ten copies of the Book of Mormon and taught two discussions."

I couldn't believe my eyes or ears. This was the spiritless young man who only a few days before had wanted to quit. Now he was bubbling over with spirit and enthusiasm that not even a brush with death could dampen. I said jokingly: "Elder, lie back down; you're dying."

What wrought the miracle? Why had the Spirit returned to the missionary? It was simply a matter of working and courting and courting and working. The spirit of the missionary's calling returned with strength and vigor because he had opened the way by remembering, desiring, studying, praying, and working.

Retaining the Spirit of a Calling

If we discover that our work is losing its zest and appeal, we can rest assured that one of the five steps above has been neglected. To get back on track, we need to refresh our remembering, direct our desire, shore up our study, persist with our prayers, and warm up our work.

I love an expression by Elder Parley P. Pratt, who said of his calling: "If I had been set to turn the world over, to dig down a mountain, to go to the ends of the earth, or traverse the deserts of Arabia, it would have been easier than to have undertaken to rest, while the priesthood was upon me. I have received the holy anointing, and I can never rest till the last enemy is conquered, death destroyed, and truth reigns triumphant" (Quoted by Marion G. Romney, *Conference Report,* October 1941, p. 90).

Elder Pratt's proclivity for action was not accidental. He had been up and doing, and he knew that his doing was all important. His priesthood and priesthood calling, animated by the Spirit, would not allow him to rest while there was work yet to be done.

When one reads the histories of those who launched missionary services in this dispensation, one must acknowledge that they were influenced by a compelling spirit. Why else would they leave hearth and home, family and friends, to risk life and limb in building the kingdom of God on earth? The answer is obvious; they courted the Holy Spirit, even that Spirit that prompts us to share the truth in a selfless manner.

Said Brigham Young: "I wanted to thunder and roar out the Gospel to the nations. It burned in my bones like fire pent up, so I turned my back upon Jackson County to preach the Gospel of life to the people. . . . Nothing would satisfy me but to cry abroad in the world, what the Lord was doing in the Latter-days (*Journal of Discourses,* 1:313).

Concern and Desire for Others

It seems to me that the spirit we are discussing is founded upon genuine concern for others and a sincere desire for their eternal well-being. Sometimes, this concern and desire lie dormant within us until we are faced with a threatening situation or exposed to sobering truths. Such conditions may be better understood through a newspaper account and a story.

Years ago, the city of Hobart, Tasmania, was divided by a river channel. To unite the city, a bridge was constructed at great cost to span the river. When completed, the bridge accomplished its purpose and all were pleased about its erection. However, in January of 1975, a ship with tall masts sailed through the channel and severed the bridge. The following day a newspaper account was published under the caption "Terror on the Bridge Edge." It read in part as follows:

HOBART. — A man and his wife told today of their seconds of terror in a car hanging half over the collapsed span of the Tasman Bridge with a 50–metre drop to the water below.

Mr. Frank Manley, 44, of Cambridge, his wife Sylvia, daughter Sharon, 16, and brother-in-law John Fitzgerald, 33, were driving along the mile-long bridge last night when suddenly there was no more roadway. Today, Mr. Manley, still shaking, told how his wife screamed: "Quick, there's no bridge."

Mr. Manley said: "That was it. It was too late. We were partly over the bridge — almost half the car was hanging. Sylvia scrambled out and told Sharon and John in the back seat to get out quickly. It's a two-door car and when I opened my door there was nothing — just a sheer drop. I scrambled out with my back pressed hard against the pillar of the car and eased myself back on to the crumbling roadway," Mr. Manley said.

Mrs. Manley said: "As soon as I got out I ran down the road to tell people to stop. I just ran. I didn't look back. I tried to stop this bloke in a yellow car. He was going too fast. He nearly ran me down. I screamed at him and he slammed into the back of a car beside us and pushed him over the edge so that car was hanging like ours. Then came a bus; I waved. He turned his wheel and just missed a car."

The man in the other car left teetering over the brink is Mr. Murray Ling, a Beelerive. He, his wife and two children were crossing the bridge when the lights went out. Mr. Ling said: "I knew something bad must have happened and I slowed down. I stopped three feet from the gap, I think. I got out and started waving and a car came through fast in another lane. He thumped into another car, flew past and dropped over the edge."

I ask, why did Mrs. Manley and Mr. Ling throw all caution to the wind and race toward the oncoming traffic and raise their warning voices? Why did they place their lives in jeopardy? I believe they acted as they did because their spirits were awakened by the threat at hand; and, their spirits called out to the others, hoping that lives could be saved. Why not? Aren't we all the children of God? Isn't he the Father of all Spirits? (See Hebrews 12:9.) Are we not brothers and sisters all and required to be our brothers' keepers?

We are all members of the family of Adam (see 2 Nephi 9:21). The twin concepts of the fatherhood of God and the brotherhood of man are real. And, yes, there are inborn spiritual ties between all people that become apparent especially in moments of danger and when bridges come falling down.

We are called to raise a warning voice to all who are driving recklessly toward spiritual destruction. Like the motorists on the Tasman Bridge, many will be drowned in the waters of sin unless someone invites them to repent. And, like Mrs. Manley and Mr. Ling, those who are called to the work and filled with the Spirit stand in the gap, wave their hands, and call out "stop," because the spark of divinity within them will not allow them to stand by as idle spectators and watch others — their brothers and sisters — suffer spiritual death. Such expressed concern and desires for others, even perfect strangers, is the true spirit of gospel service!

Shared Virtue

There is an interesting exchange between a perceptive woman and a prospective monk in one of Sir Arthur Conan Doyle's stories. The conversation proceeds as follows:

> "God help me! I am the weakest of the weak," groaned Alleyne. "I pray that I may have more strength."
>
> "And to what end?" she asked sharply. "If you are, as I understand, to shut yourself forever in your cell within the four walls of the abbey, then of what use would it be were your prayer to be answered?"
>
> "The use of my own salvation."
>
> She turned from him with a pretty shrug and wave. "Is that all?" she said. "Then you are no better than Father Christopher and the rest of them. Your own, your own, even your own! My father is the king's man, and when he rides into the press of fight he is not thinking ever of the saving of his own poor body; he recks little enough if he leave it on the field. Why then should you, who are soldiers of the Spirit, be ever moping or hiding in cell or in cave, with minds full of your own concerns, while the world, which you should be mending, is going on its way, and neither sees nor hears you? Were ye all as thoughtless of your own souls as the soldier is of his body, ye would be of more avail to the souls of others."
>
> "There is sooth in what you say, lady," Alleyne answered; "and yet I scarce can see what you would have the clergy and the church to do."
>
> "I would have them live as others and do men's work in the world, preaching by their lives rather than their

41

words. I would have them come forth from their lonely places, mix with the borel folks, feel the pains and the pleasures, the cares and the rewards, the temptings and the stirrings of the common people. Let them toil and swinken, and labor, and plough the land, and take wives to themselves—"

"Alas! alas!" cried Alleyne aghast, "you have surely sucked this poison from the man Wicliffe, of whom I have heard such evil things."

"Nay, I know him not. I have learned it by looking from my own chamber window and marking these poor monks of the priory, their weary life, their profitless round. I have asked myself if the best which can be done with virtue is to shut it within high walls as though it were some savage creature. If the good will lock themselves up, and if the wicked will still wander free, then alas for the world!" ("The White Company," *The Works of A. Conan Doyle* [Roslyn, New York: Black's Readers Service Company, n.d.], p. 222.)

Many provocative truths emerge in this conversation. I emphasize only three: (1) those who are called to service in the Church must be "soldiers of the Spirit" and give freely of themselves if they expect to be "of more avail to the souls of others"; (2) those who know and live the truth have virtue that must be shared, else "the wicked will still wander free, then alas the world"; and, (3) all who are possessed of the spirit of their callings will preach, live righteously, and share virtue freely for "the use of [their] own salvation" and the salvation of others.

Conclusion

Elder Marion G. Romney stated: "No person whose soul is illuminated by the burning Spirit of God can in this world of sin and dense darkness remain passive. He is driven by an irresistible urge to fit himself to be an active agent of

God in furthering righteousness and in freeing the lives and minds of men from the bondage of sin" (*Conference Report,* October 1941, p. 89).

I can attest that there is an "irresistible urge" and a lifting spirit associated with service in the Church. I'm convinced that each time we walk our roads to Emmaus with those we are called to serve, talking and opening up the scriptures to them, our eyes are opened to added truths and our hearts burn brighter. I'm convinced that each time we extend the right hand to the lame in body and spirit at our Gates Beautiful and lift people up, we walk a little straighter and praise God with greater fervor. I'm convinced that each time we visit our Jacob's wells and invite friends to drink of living waters, our thirst is quenched and we draw closer to the Savior of the world.

If I were granted one wish, it would be similar to President Brown's. My wish, however, would apply to all members of the Church, not just the full-time missionaries. Within my heart is the compelling desire that all members of the Church, young and old, be influenced and motivated by the special spirit that accompanies the sharing and the living of the gospel of Jesus Christ. Would that all Latter-day Saints had intimate and continuous association with that spirit!

May God bless you to court, catch, and retain the spirit of your calling. May the Spirit of the Lord walk with you daily and give you the companionship that brings unspeakable joy.

Chapter Five

Becoming Men and Women of God

You may be wondering why *you* were the one called to fill your position. Perhaps you are uneasy, worrying about your lack of training or experience. I understand well the questions and doubts that may be running through your mind. Most people go through this same type of trial, especially at the beginning of their calling.

First, I would advise you to heed Paul's words to Timothy: "Let no man despise thy youth [in your calling]. . . . Give attendance to reading, to exhortation, to doctrine. Neglect not the gift that is in thee. . . . Take heed unto thyself, and . . . save thyself, and them that hear thee" (1 Timothy 4:12–16).

God does use the seemingly "weak things of the world" to accomplish his purposes (see D&C 1:19). You may feel inexperienced now, but with the help of the Lord, you can become one of his strong advocates.

Second, don't allow your doubts or questions to cast a

shadow over your divine calling. No, you probably haven't received a degree in religious studies or organizational behavior. You probably have, however, enjoyed the divine tutoring of parents, concerned priesthood leaders, and an army of Church teachers. You may also have grown through auxiliary programs, seminary, and other classes. Like Amos of old, you have been taken by the Lord and given a message to proclaim, a task to perform (see Amos 7:10–17). So don't apologize for your lack of formal training. In time, you can become all or more than you imagined, if you apply yourself fully to your calling.

I counsel you strongly not to be persuaded or influenced by those who question your faithfulness and determination to live the gospel. Perhaps your standard of gospel living is higher than the standards of those who live about you. It should be, for you enjoy a fulness of the gospel that most people don't. But, because I know of the worldly landmines and pitfalls that endanger the safety and success of those called to serve, I want to discuss some thoughts about becoming a man or woman of Christ.

A Personal Test

Soon after my graduation from high school, I served in the U.S. Army. World War II was in progress, and virtually all men between the ages of eighteen and thirty were serving in the military. I had spent little time away from home, so the army experience was my first real exposure to many worldly influences.

The rigorous basic training program was easy for me because I was young and in excellent physical condition. While most recruits complained about the long marches, I asked for more. Daily calisthenics, obstacle courses, and other exercises were dreaded by nearly all; however, I ran through each as if it were a game.

Most of my associates lived for the weekends when they could leave the camp and go into town. Their reasons for going into the nearby cities were made evident on Monday mornings in the form of hangovers and other miseries related to licentious living. I was content to remain at camp and to spend my time in the recreational hall, library, and chapel.

On one occasion, I was persuaded to join a group on a weekend excursion. I was told that the itinerary for the day included some sightseeing, a lunch, and a movie. I was promised that there would be no carousing. All the men knew that I was a Latter-day Saint and that I was deeply committed to the moral standards of the Church.

Upon reaching the city, we visited a place or two of historical significance and ate lunch. Then the inevitable happened—the group turned toward a bar and a house of ill-repute. I refused to enter these dens of iniquity, and I openly expressed my anger over the broken promises of my associates.

As I walked away with the determination to return to camp, my companions taunted me by shouting, "When are you going to grow up?" "When will you stop being a sissy and a religious fanatic?" "When are you going to be a man?"

Manliness

It was obvious that my associates were worldly people who equated manliness with the ability to swill liquor, the ability to blow tobacco smoke out of all the facial cavities, and the inclination to sow one's wild oats like some animal on the street. They were "Malboro Men," "Lucky Lager Lads," and "macho men" who, like Old Scratch himself, wanted me to be miserable like unto themselves (see 2 Nephi 2:27).

Perhaps you too have been tested as I was tested on that

occasion. Perhaps you too have been subjected to ridicule or derision simply because you were determined to live in accord with the whisperings of the Spirit, with the dictates of your conscience, and in harmony with the truths you have been taught.

Perhaps you too have learned to appreciate the feelings undergirding this scripture: "Wo unto them that call evil good, and good evil, that put darkness for light, and light for darkness, that put bitter for sweet, and sweet for bitter!" (2 Nephi 15:20).

A New Twist

In recent years, the evil one has been pushed into a corner. The myth of the Marlboro Man is going up in smoke with the aid of science and religion. Much of the luck related to lager and other strong drinks has gone down the drain. And, to some extent, the "machoness" of carnal living has suffered some disillusionment.

Oh, the battle isn't over; there are still some who equate manliness with liquor, tobacco, illicit sex, and long hair. But, it seems that Satan has launched a new attack upon young people in his diabolical effort to enslave their souls.

This new attack is soft, subtle, and serious. I refer to it as a "new twist" because it takes truth and turns it ever so slightly until it becomes gross error. It was introduced to me by a full-time missionary who observed some of the rules and commandments; he worked part of the time; and on occasion he displayed respect for his calling.

However, when I asked why he seemed satisfied with a mediocre or "spotty" performance, he replied, "I'm deliberately holding back because I don't want to become too religious." He added, "I want to go home as a 'balanced man.' "

Balance

A cold chill went through my body when I heard these damning words, for I realized that Lucifer was now preying upon the young — even the young people of the Church — with perverted thinking that fools even some of the elect. In the name of balance, he warns against becoming too good, too honest, too righteous, and too saintly. And, he does all of this as if a little of this and a little of that is the preferred way — the balanced way — to live one's life.

Satan's Song

It is the same old song that has been sung by Satan's swingers since the days of Adam. He may have changed the tune, but the lyrics are the same:

Satan's Song

You should give a measure, grab a measure,
In this world of strife.
You should seek some pleasure, shun some pleasure,
And live the balanced life.
You must labor a little, loaf a little,
But don't do the best you can.
You must obey a law, omit a law,
And become the balanced man.

(Carlos E. Asay)

With such lyrics, Satan pacifies and lulls people into a false sense of security until they say: "Eat, drink, and be merry, for tomorrow we die; and it shall be well with us. . . . Nevertheless, fear God — he will justify in committing a little sin; yea, lie a little, take the advantage of one because of his words, dig a pit for thy neighbor; there is no harm in this; and do all these things, for tomorrow we die; and if it so be that we are guilty, God will beat us with a few stripes, and at last we shall be saved in the kingdom of God" (2 Nephi 28:7–8). Nephi wrote of such people:

48

They are led, that in many instances they do err because they are taught by the precepts of men. . . .

And others will he pacify, and lull them away into carnal security, that they will say: All is well in Zion; yea, Zion prospereth, all is well — and thus the devil cheateth their souls, and leadeth them away carefully down to hell.

And behold, others he flattereth away, and telleth them there is no hell; and he saith unto them: I am no devil, for there is none — and thus he whispereth in their ears, until he grasps them with his awful chains, from whence there is no deliverance. . . .

Therefore, wo be unto him that is at ease in Zion! (2 Nephi 28:14, 21–22, 24).

Awful Chains

The "awful chains" with which the devil binds his subjects are not placed around the wrist or neck of the so-called "balanced" man or woman all at once. They begin as a single flaxen thread and grow into chains that become progressively more and more controlling.

You see, Satan is the founder of works of darkness, and he does, as mentioned in the Book of Mormon, lead the balanced man and woman "by the neck with a flaxen cord, until he bindeth them with his strong cords forever" (2 Nephi 26:22).

The Real Issue

The real issue is: Can a man or woman be too religious or too righteous? If religion is defined as that pure religion described in the Epistle of James, the answer to the question is an emphatic no! To say otherwise is to say that a man or woman can become too Christlike (see James 1:27).

In one of my favorite stories, two men seeking adventure rode by a church early in the morning. Both had been exposed to the life of a monk — both had been trained in a monastery. One, remembering that they had forgotten to pray, said: "What! not one word of prayer before God's own open house? How can ye hope for His blessing upon the day?"

"My friend," said the other, "I have prayed so much during the last two months . . . that I feel that I have over-prayed myself."

"How can a man have too much religion?" cried [the first] earnestly. "It is the one thing that availeth. A man is but a beast as he lives from day to day, eating and drinking, breathing and sleeping. It is only when he raises himself, and concerns himself with the immortal spirit within him, that he becomes in truth a man. Bethink ye how sad a thing it would be that the blood of the Redeemer should be spilled to no purpose" (Sir Arthur Conan Doyle, "The White Company," *Works of A. Conan Doyle,* p. 181).

This inspired thought reminds us that the life of an animal is ruled by the appetites of the flesh. It also reminds us that the spirits within us are the offspring of God and should be the ruling forces in our lives. Our task is to rise above the level of beasts and to become the true reflection of him who gave us life.

Be Men — Be Women

You will recall the stirring counsel Father Lehi gave his sons as he approached death. Among other things, he declared: "Arise from the dust, my sons, and be men, and be determined in one mind and in one heart, united in all things, that ye may not come down into captivity. . . . Awake, my sons; put on the armor of righteousness. Shake off the chains with which ye are bound, and come forth out of obscurity, and arise from the dust" (2 Nephi 1:21, 23).

Lehi knew that "all flesh is of the dust" (Jacob 2:21). He also knew that carnal tendencies must be overcome and the

Spirit allowed to control one's life. Hence, he pleaded with his sons to grow up in spiritual things and to become men — men of the Spirit.

Jacob, the son of Lehi, learned well from his father, for he wrote, "To be carnally-minded is death, and to be spiritually-minded is life eternal" (2 Nephi 9:39).

Fruits of the Flesh and the Spirit

It is not difficult to determine whether one's life is controlled by the flesh or by the Spirit, for as the Savior taught, "By their fruits ye shall know them" (Matthew 7:20). The Apostle Paul identifies the fruits, or "works of the flesh," as "adultery, fornication, uncleanness, lasciviousness, idolatry, witchcraft, hatred, variance, emulations, wrath, strife, seditions, heresies, envyings, murders, drunkenness, revellings, and such like" (Galatians 5:19–21).

In contrast, his list of the fruits of the Spirit includes "love, joy, peace, longsuffering, gentleness, goodness, faith, meekness, temperance: against such there is no law" (Galatians 5:22–23).

Paul concludes by saying, "If we live in the Spirit, let us also walk in the Spirit" (Galatians 5:25). He might have added, "If we live and walk in the Spirit, we shall be men and women of God."

There is no balance in living on the fringes of our faith, with one foot in Zion and one foot in Babylon. We cannot be sinners part of the time and saints part of the time. We cannot be servants of the Lord one moment and people of the world the next. It won't work. It smacks of hypocrisy. Those who attempt to do so teeter on the brink of disaster. As James stated, "A double minded man is unstable in all his ways" (James 1:8).

Occasionally, I hear of some young people who rejoice when they leave home for the first time and who feel inclined to experiment with worldly influences once they are beyond the sight of parents or other authority figures. They regard their "freedom" as license to stretch the commandments, test the waters of sin, and engage in questionable practices. Usually, those who use "liberty for an occasion to the flesh" do so thinking, I will only do it once or twice, and I can repent later. Such misled people, however, fail to recognize the binding nature of drugs, other stimulants, and undesirable habits. They forget that fire from any source burns or destroys and leaves ugly and sometimes irreparable scars. (See Galatians 5:13.)

Hot or Cold?

We must also remember full salvation does not come by giving 50 percent and withholding 50 percent, on the pretext of living a balanced Christian life. God, through his divine grace, gave us his all — even his Beloved Son. In return, we are expected to give our all, not just a part or token performance of goodness.

There is a story about a man who was asked, "Are you a Christian?" He replied, "I is in spots." What an awful admission of inconsistency and hypocrisy!

Christ had little patience for hypocrites or part-time Christians who "pay tithe of mint and anise and cummin, and have omitted the weightier matters of the law" (Matthew 23:23).

God warns us: "I know thy works, that thou art neither cold nor hot: I would thou wert cold or hot. So then because thou art lukewarm, and neither cold nor hot, I will spue thee out of my mouth" (Revelation 3:15–16).

I have always been intrigued by the doctrine taught in the 15th chapter of Mosiah:

> Abinadi said unto them: I would that ye should un-

derstand that God himself shall come down among the children of men, and shall redeem his people.

And because he dwelleth in flesh he shall be called the Son of God, and having subjected the flesh to the will of the Father, being the Father and the Son—

The Father, because he was conceived by the power of God; and the Son, because of the flesh; thus becoming the Father and Son. . . .

And thus *the flesh becoming subject to the Spirit,* or the Son to the Father, being one God, suffereth temptation, and yielded not to the temptation, but suffereth himself to be mocked, and scourged, and cast out, and disowned by his people.

And after all this, after working many mighty miracles among the children of men, he shall be led, yea, even as Isaiah said, as sheep before the shearer is dumb, so he opened not his mouth.

Yea, even so he shall be led, crucified, and slain, the flesh becoming subject even unto death, *the will of the Son being swallowed up in the will of the Father.* (Mosiah 15:1–3, 5–7; italics added.)

I underscore these words: "The flesh becoming subject to the Spirit . . . the will of the Son being swallowed up in the will of the Father."

Christ grew grace by grace and lived the perfect life. The divine spirit within him — not the flesh — gained control of his soul. In time, he became all that his Father wanted him to become, and he did all that his Father wanted him to do. Should we not strive to do the same?

Christ did not seek to obtain a balance or a 50–50 relationship between the spirit and the flesh. To have done so would have caused him to fall short of his divine calling and his Father's expectations.

Becoming Saints

One of the most significant passages in holy writ tells us how to become a saint. Please note that no reference is made to a balance between the flesh (the "natural man") and the spirit: "The natural man is an enemy to God, and has been from the fall of Adam, and will be, forever and ever, unless he yields to the enticings of the Holy Spirit, and putteth off the natural man and becometh a saint through the atonement of Christ the Lord, and becometh as a child, submissive, meek, humble, patient, full of love, willing to submit to all things which the Lord seeth fit to inflict upon him, even as a child doth submit to his father" (Mosiah 3:19).

We must yield to the enticings of the Holy Spirit; we must learn to submit to the will of the Lord; and, we must cultivate the fruits of the Spirit — if we hope to become saints through the atonement of Christ the Lord.

Becoming Real Servants of God

The process of becoming saints, men and women of God, is illustrated beautifully in this true account from the life of J. Willard Marriott:

> There were twenty-five missionaries on the train bound for New York and the Eastern States Mission. . . . They came from nearly every state in the Rocky Mountain west. One of them Bill [Willard] never forgot, a slender, sunburnt young sheep-rancher from southern Utah. He swore it was the first train he'd ever seen, and Bill believed him. All the others wore their somber missionary clothes; he came aboard wearing a black suit, but with it a plaid shirt, curled-brim cowboy hat, and high-heeled cowboy boots. In New York, he refused to part with his hat or his boots. He would stutter and stumble through a street-corner meeting and finally give up in red-faced confusion.
>
> A year later, Bill saw him preaching to a crowd on the New Haven Green. He wore white shirt, black tie, and celluloid collar, black suit and shoes, and in his right hand

held a black derby. His face was paler, but he spoke confidently and forcefully. The crowd listened intently.

The transformation was amazing. "How'd you do it?" Bill asked after the meeting.

The sheepherder shrugged. "I just realized one day how raw I was, how poorly equipped to do the Lord's work. So I buckled down and changed my ways and my outlook, and studied hard, and began to do not what I wanted to do, but what the Lord asked me to do. I still have far to go. But I've started."

Later Bill said this proved to him for all time the tremendous change that true religion can have on the life of an individual who lives close to the Lord. (Robert O'Brien, *Marriott* [Salt Lake City: Deseret Book Company, 1977], p. 74.)

What wrought the miracle in this instance? How was the sheepherder transformed into a true undershepherd for the Lord? Answers to these questions are cradled in these words:

"I just realized one day how raw I was, how poorly equipped to do the Lord's work."

"I buckled down."

"[I] changed my ways."

"[I changed] my outlook."

"[I] studied hard."

"[I] began to do not what I wanted to do, but what the Lord asked me to do."

If we hope to become men and women of Christ, we must be born of the Spirit and be "quickened in the inner man" (see Moses 6:65). This process of sanctification occurs as we "fast and pray oft, and . . . wax stronger in [our] humility, and firmer and firmer in the faith of Christ, unto the filling [our] souls with joy and consolation, yea, even to the purifying and the sanctification of [our] hearts, which sanctification cometh because of [our] yielding [our] hearts unto God" (see Helaman 3:35).

Moreover, to become all that we hope to become we must: "hold upon the word of God, which is quick and powerful, which shall divide asunder all the cunning and the snares and the wiles of the devil, and lead the man of Christ in a strait and narrow course across that everlasting gulf of misery which is prepared to engulf the wicked" (Helaman 3:29).

Conclusion

Elijah challenged a people by asking, "How long halt ye between two opinions? if the Lord be God, follow him: but if Baal, then follow him" (1 Kings 18:21).

We must make a decision and stand our ground, for as Christ taught, "No man can serve two masters: for either he will hate the one, and love the other; or else he will hold to the one, and despise the other. Ye cannot serve God and mammon" (Matthew 6:24).

Said Alma to a confused and divided son, "Wickedness never was happiness" (Alma 41:10). He could have added, "Wickedness never was manliness."

So, my advice to you is to do all within your power to become a man or woman of Christ. Don't be misled by the miserable voices that sing Satan's deadly lullabies. Don't heed the scoffings of the fools who equate a balanced life with the life of a hypocrite. Seek always to become a saint — a saint of the living God. Seek to become a servant of Christ, for it was he who instructed, "What manner of men ought ye to be? Verily I say unto you, even as I am" (3 Nephi 27:27).

Our challenge is to withstand the taunts of worldly men and women, who would have us become creatures of the flesh, and to accept the invitation of the "Master Man" and become creatures of the Spirit. By so doing, we will find happiness in this life and abiding joy hereafter. God help us always in that noble quest to become men and women of Christ.

Chapter Six

Yielding Yourself as an Instrument of Righteousness

If you are faithful in your calling, the Spirit will guide you in it. Few experiences in life are quite so sweet as those involving strokes of inspiration, floods of new ideas or thoughts never before entertained, and powers of expression that seem to penetrate the innermost recesses of the soul. Such occasions verify that there is a source of light and goodness beyond ourselves and that we can tap that source and become its instrument, if we live and serve righteously.

Knights of Old

As a small boy in grammar school, I had a teacher who made King Arthur and the Knights of the Round Table come alive for me. She caused me to become so obsessed with stories of knights that I played and dreamed that I was one.

One evening I dreamed that I was a white knight on a white horse riding over the greens of England. Suddenly, without warning, a knight dressed in black armor and mounted on a black horse appeared at the edge of the forest. We measured each other carefully, lowered our lances, and charged at full gallop. The lances struck target, and both of us were knocked off our steeds.

I scrambled to my feet, knowing that we would draw our swords and that hand-to-hand combat was imminent. Fear gripped my heart as I saw my opponent rushing toward me flashing a long, gleaming sword. Instinctively, I reached to my side and drew forth from the scabbard my weapon. That is when the dream turned into a nightmare! For in my hand was a tiny dagger—not a long, gleaming sword. I woke up in a cold sweat screaming for help.

Many times since that nightmarish experience, I have wondered about the serviceability of the Saints. When God calls us to serve, are we positioned in the scabbard and ready to be drawn? When the Lord draws us forth as his instrument in combating evil forces, what does he have in his hand—a long, gleaming sword or a dinky dagger?

Shared Opportunities

At one time I wondered why God did not take matters into his own hands and guarantee the salvation of all people. I knew that God was omnipotent and could, if he so willed, thunder his word over the earth and blaze his message across the skies with such convincing power that everyone would join the Church. I also knew he could build all the temples needed, perform all the family history research required, and do all else—single-handedly, letter perfect, and without any wasted motion. Yes, I knew that God could do it all by simple command without the help or intrusion of weak mortals.

As my understanding of the gospel of Jesus Christ expanded, I saw the folly of a "one-man show." I realized that if Heavenly Father took matters into his own hands and performed all the missionary, temple, and other Church services, he would (1) offend our agency in a manner similar to what Lucifer proposed before the world was formed (see Moses 4:1–3) and (2) deprive us of sanctifying experiences, just as impatient, perfectionist parents deprive their children of growth when they push the children aside and do all the work themselves. These and other gospel insights led me to the conclusion that an all-wise and loving Father involves his children in his work so they may grow, learn, and become like him.

Opposite Forces

From the very beginning, our Heavenly Father has worked through his children in fulfilling his holy purposes. It was through his Only Begotten Son that the Atonement was wrought. Another son, Adam, became the father of the whole human family. Moses led the children of Israel out of bondage. A modern Joseph became the prophet of the Restoration. All of these leaders served as agents, or instruments, in the hands of God in helping to fulfill his avowed purpose of bringing "to pass the immortality and eternal life of man" (Moses 1:39). Each was sanctified and assumed attributes of the Father in the process.

Other children of God listened to another voice, a dissident voice, and made themselves instruments of that outcast Satan. This was done in fulfillment of Lucifer's pledge "to deceive and to blind men, and to lead them captive at his will" (Moses 4:4), for he had warned that he would fight his battles and extend his rule through those who loved darkness more than light.

Satan used the hands of Cain in committing murder (see Moses 5:17–35); he used Korihor as his voice in preaching anti-Christ doctrine (see Alma 30:6–21); and he abused Sherem's learned nature and perfect knowledge of language by having him sow seeds of doubt among the Nephites (see Jacob 7:1–20). In each of these instances, Cain, Korihor, or Sherem yielded himself to Satan and became an instrument of unrighteousness. Each was abandoned in the end by his tempter and allowed to go down in bitter defeat (see Alma 30:60).

Yield Yourselves to God

The Apostle Paul understood clearly the life-and-death struggle for the souls of men. He was aware of the enlistment programs of both sides — the Savior and his Saints, and Lucifer and his legions. Therefore, he issued this warning to the Romans, "Neither yield ye your members as instruments of unrighteousness unto sin: but yield yourselves unto God, as those that are alive from the dead, and your members as instruments of righteousness unto God" (Romans 6:13). He added, "Know ye not, that to whom ye yield yourselves servants to obey, his servants ye are to whom ye obey; whether of sin unto death, or of obedience unto righteousness?" (Romans 6:16).

To yield is to give or submit oneself. So the first issue is, are you positioned in the scabbard of righteousness and ready to be drawn by the hand of God? Alma and the sons of Mosiah, through disobedience, allowed themselves to slip into the wrong sheath. An evil hand drew them forth and caused them to become an impediment to the Church of God. This period of subjection to Satan was later referred to by Alma as the "gall of bitterness," "bonds of iniquity," and "the darkest abyss" (Mosiah 27:29).

After a miraculous conversion, Alma and his friends changed scabbards. They confessed their sins, tried to repair the injuries they had made, and published peace. And, according to the record, "they were instruments in the hands of God in bringing many to the knowledge of the truth, yea, to the knowledge of their Redeemer" (Mosiah 27:36).

The slide into Satan's scabbard begins with little and seemingly harmless transgressions. It may start with a cigarette, a suggestive thought, an off-color story, one alcoholic drink, a so-called white lie, or even one X-rated movie. Gradually, however, the sins mount in number and seriousness until one finds himself Satan-ward. Each wrongdoing molds the transgressor's hilt to fit the hand of Lucifer.

In contrast, properly directed faith, repentance, and well-doing guides one into the scabbard strapped to the side of Deity. The young person who cultivates a love for the scriptures, attends church, becomes involved in service projects, prays daily and honestly, and who honors loving parents is positioning himself or herself for righteous service. A state of useful readiness is achieved virtue by virtue as the hilt of the instrument and the hand of God become molded as one.

Gleaming Swords or Dinky Daggers?

Now, the second issue: When the Lord draws you forth to wage his battles, does he have in his hand a long, gleaming sword? If I were a knight and I was preparing for combat, I would select carefully the tools of my trade. At the top of my list of tools would be a strong, sharp, and gleaming sword. I would want one that was perfectly balanced and honed to a fine cutting edge. It would be of the finest steel and fitted so perfectly to my hand that it felt like an extension of my arm. I would not want to be hindered by a small, useless weapon that I could have little confidence in. A long, gleaming sword, however, would reflect light and power; it would stir confidence in the heart of its user and strike fear into the heart of its intended target.

Strong, Sharp, Clean

To observers in Jerusalem of a former day, Peter may have appeared to be a small, useless weapon as he denied Christ thrice near the high priest's palace (see Matthew 26:69–75). But when the converted Peter stood before the Jews on the day of Pentecost, he testified with conviction and the power of a gleaming sword, placing himself in the hands of God and winning the souls of three thousand people (see Acts 2).

The mettle of the man Peter did not come automatically and without effort. Peter was subjected to trials and temptations and all else referred to as the "refiner's fire." The heat of opposition did not consume him; it served only to burn out the impurities and weaknesses and to leave the refined and pure metal. He emerged from the furnace of affliction as a polished, strong sword of righteousness. His iron strength of character carried him through to the end of his mission.

Peter, after the day of Pentecost, was a man with a cutting edge. He exhibited a sharpness of mind that enabled him to bear witness of the risen Christ. It is recorded that on one occasion his words "cut to the heart" those who sought to slay him (see Acts 5:33). Undoubtedly, such sharpness of mind was the result of much study, fasting, and prayer.

We are taught that miracles are performed and revelation received through clean vessels of the Lord (see 3 Nephi 8:1). Peter's cleanliness of soul gained him deliverance from prison at the hands of angels. It provided him power to heal the sick and raise Dorcas from death (see Acts 9:36–43). And his purity made it possible for him to see a vision that led to the extension of the gospel to the Gentiles.

The saving virtue of a sword is related to its strength,

sharpness, and cleanliness, and the hand that guides it. Is it not the same with people?

A Prayer

I thrill when I hear of young people who keep themselves clean, pure, and pointed for full-time missions and temple marriages. Their "obedience unto righteousness" is an inspiration to all. Surely these valiant ones will receive wages of the one "they list to obey," which is all that the Father hath (see D&C 29:45; 84:38).

I pray that the members of the Church, particularly those with callings from the Lord, will understand the necessity of becoming active participants and not simply spectators in the cause of truth. I pray that they will keep themselves God-ward, positioned in his scabbard and ready to be drawn into action. Moreover, I pray that they will seek strength of character, sharpness of mind, and cleanliness of soul so as to become gleaming swords of righteousness. By doing this, there will be no embarrassment, no disappointment, and no nightmare when he draws them out in battling the powers of darkness.

May God bless you as you grow in his service. Do yield yourself as an instrument of righteousness and "war a good warfare" against the powers of darkness, just as Paul counseled Timothy (1 Timothy 1:18).

Chapter Seven

Developing Good Habits and Noble Character

Usually when people receive new callings from the Lord, they resolve to improve themselves, to acquire good habits so they can better serve. This resolve should be high on the list for all who enter the work of the Lord. I say this because good habits are the basis of the pattern of behavior that distinguishes a devoted servant of God.

Since habits and character are so interrelated, I desire to share with you some thoughts that may be of help as you develop your abilities.

Binding Threads

I once conducted a demonstration before an audience at Brigham Young University. I invited two newly called missionaries to assist me. Each young man was invited to extend his wrists toward me so that I might handcuff him with flaxen thread. The first missionary, the smaller of the two, I bound with a single strand. I said that this single strand of thread represented one undesirable habit. The second missionary, a rather tall and muscular person, I bound with twenty strands of the flaxen thread. As I wrapped the thread around his wrists, I identified each strand as a bad habit, such as lying, stealing, cheating, profaning, using tobacco, drinking alcohol, procrastinating, and so on.

Once the threads were in place, I asked the missionaries to free themselves of the binding threads. The missionary bound with a single strand broke the string with little effort. My other captive, however, despite his size and strength, could not break the cords that bound him tight. He strained so hard that the thread began to cut into his wrists. Blood appeared on the surface of his skin, and I had to stop him from straining further.

We concluded from the demonstration three things: (1) a single bad habit has limited restricting power; (2) a number of bad habits, one piled upon another, have great and almost limitless power; and (3) that all bad habits should be broken or overcome and not allowed to grow into strong cords.

Chains of Habit

"The chains of habit," said Samuel Johnson, "are too small to be felt until they are too strong to be broken."

Plato, it is said, once rebuked a person for engaging in a gambling game. When the person protested that he had only played for a trifle, Plato replied, "The habit is not a trifle" (*The Home Book of Quotations*, selected and arranged by Burton Stevenson, 8th ed. [New York: Dodd, Mead and Company, 1956], p. 845).

When I taught at BYU, I worked with students who fitted, floated, or failed. Those who fitted came with purpose, high resolve, and good work habits. Those who floated appeared on the scene for a semester or two and faded away to something less challenging when their grades finally caught up with them. Those who failed lacked the commitment and discipline required of a person in an institution of higher learning.

It seemed to me that most of the failures were shackled by poor habits. Some were not in the habit of attending class regularly; some were not in the habit of reading required texts; some were habitually late in submitting assignments; some were not in the habit of budgeting time and energies; and some were not even conditioned to work. In all too many cases, so it seemed to me, one weakness seemed to breed upon another, and what appeared at first to be a flaxen habit proved to be a strong inhibiting cord.

A Spanish proverb says: "Habits are at first cobwebs, then cables." I suspect that most students go to school with pure intent. They register, select their courses of study, and attend their classes with high hopes of attaining declared goals. But, when they become careless, when they permit resolve to sag, slouchy habits appear, and academic anemia sets in. This malady comes web by web until learning and growing are choked off by the cables of intellectual inactivity.

Bundles of Habits

More than a decade ago, a young man wrote BYU President Ernest L. Wilkinson to ask what he should do to become a successful leader. President Wilkinson responded with some wise counsel, including this quotation from philosopher and psychologist William James:

> The hell to be endured hereafter, of which theology tells, is no worse than the hell we make for ourselves in this world by habitually fashioning our characters in the wrong way. Could the young but realize how soon they will become mere walking bundles of habits, they would give more heed to their conduct while in the plastic state. We are spinning our fates, good or evil, and never to be

undone. Every smallest stroke of virtue or of vice leaves its never so little scar. The drunken Rip Van Winkle, in Jefferson's play, excuses himself for every fresh dereliction by saying, "I won't count this time!" Well! he may not count it, and a kind Heaven may not count it; but it is being counted none the less. Down among his nerve-cells and fibres the molecules are counting it, registering and storing it up to be used against him when the next temptation comes. Nothing we ever do is, in strict scientific literalness, wiped out. Of course, this has its good side as well as its bad one. As we become permanent drunkards by so many separate drinks, so we become saints in the moral, and authorities and experts in the practical and scientific spheres, by so many separate acts and hours of work. Let no youth have any anxiety about the upshot of his education, whatever the line of it may be. If he keep faithfully busy each hour of the working-day, he may safely leave the final result to itself. He can with perfect certainty count on waking up some fine morning, to find himself one of the competent ones of his generation, in whatever pursuit he may have singled out. (Letter from Ernest L. Wilkinson to Bryce V. Redd, March 2, 1971, pp. 2–3. Quoted from James, William, *The Principles of Psychology,* Great Books of the Western World, vol. 53 [Chicago: Encyclopaedia Britannica, 1952], p. 83.)

I would remind you and other "walking bundles of habits" that there is a relationship between thoughts, actions, habits, and characters. After the language of the Bible we might well say: "Thought begat Action; and Action took unto himself Habit; and Character was born of Habit; and Character was expressed through Personality. And, Character and Personality lived after the manner of their parents."

A more conventional way of linking these is found in the words of C. A. Hill: "We sow our thoughts, and we reap our actions; we sow our actions, and we reap our habits;

we sow our habits, and we reap our characters; we sow our characters, and we reap our destiny" (*Home Book of Quotations*, p. 845).

Missionary Character Born of Habit

The power of habit is especially evident in the lives of missionaries because they are in full-time service to the Lord. The true "missionary character," I feel, is the sum of all the good habits acquired through selfless day-by-day service and obedient living. It is molded slowly as the ambassador of righteousness shares the gospel of Jesus Christ and seeks to save souls.

As missionaries completed their work in the Texas North Mission, where I served, I would invite them to sit down, reflect, and list all of the habits they felt they had acquired during their terms of service. Most lists would include phrases like these:

The habit of rising and retiring early.

The habit of praying frequently.

The habit of studying the scriptures regularly.

The habit of goal-setting.

The habit of planning.

The habit of exercising daily.

The habit of working hard and consistently.

When the lists were complete, I would ask the missionaries to identify those habits they felt they should break and discard upon their return home from missionary service. Nearly all the missionaries would eye their lists carefully and respond something like this: "President, I can see only one habit I can afford to place aside."

"What is that?" I would ask.

Invariably the missionary would conclude, "I can drop my daily tracting."

I never objected to the cessation of the tracting habit.

But, I did plead for a retention of all the other habits relating to the missionary character. It seemed foolish to me that a young man or woman would invest precious months in the acquisition of something so wonderful as a missionary character and then return home and allow it to slip away.

Habit Formation

If character is truly born of habit—and it is—it is vital that all of us understand the process of habit formation. Not only will this process, if applied, enable us to refine our characters, but it will also assure us success in our Church service, at home, at school, or anyplace else.

I am no expert on the subject of habit. Nevertheless, I would like to share some steps I feel are involved in cultivating a desirable habit.

First, we must define the desired habit. We must identify it, verbalize it, and write it down. We should be as specific as possible. For example, we might write: "I will arise each morning at the appointed hour and prepare myself for proselyting duties." Or, "I will follow a scripture reading program faithfully and seek to become a gospel scholar."

Chances of successfully acquiring a new habit depend much upon how clearly we plant it in our minds and hearts. Fuzzy or vague resolves are usually short lived. A firm and definite declaration of intent has staying power. Joshua did not say to the children of Israel, "Choose, if you like, within the next month or so, whom ye will serve. But as for me and my house, we may, if all goes well, serve the Lord." With firm resolve and clarity of purpose he declared, "Choose you this day whom ye will serve . . . but as for me and my house, we will serve the Lord" (Joshua 24:15).

Second, we must bind ourselves to act and to honor our declared resolve. Through the Prophet Joseph Smith, the Lord taught the Saints how to benefit from meetings and conferences. He commanded that the Saints meet together and instruct and edify one another; and, so that the instruction would not be lost, he asked that we bind ourselves to act. The Lord's words are, "Ye shall bind yourselves to act in all holiness before me" (D&C 43:9). I feel that we bind ourselves best to a desired action by sharing our resolve with a friend, a spouse, a bishop, or someone else who can help monitor our progress. I also feel that we find strength as we share our desires with God and beg for divine assistance.

Third, we must put the new mode of conduct into operation. Just thinking about a Church calling is not sufficient. Thoughts must be supported by action. The old adage "Practice makes perfect" certainly applies in this case. And with each planned and proper action, one repetition after another, comes added strength. President Heber J. Grant often quoted this statement from Emerson: "That which we persist in doing becomes easier for us to do; not that the nature of the thing itself is changed, but that our power to do is increased" (Heber J. Grant, *Gospel Standards,* compiled by G. Homer Durham [Salt Lake City: Improvement Era, 1941], p. 355).

President Grant practiced what he preached. He tells this story of how he attempted to polish some singing skills:

> Upon my recent trip to Arizona, I asked Elders Rudger Clawson and J. Golden Kimball if they had any objections to my singing one hundred hymns that day. They took it as a joke and assured me that they would be delighted. We were on the way from Holbrook to St. Johns, a distance of about sixty miles. After I had sung about forty tunes, they assured me that if I sang the remaining sixty they would be sure to have nervous prostration. I paid no attention whatever to their appeal, but held them to their bargain and sang the full one hundred. One hundred and fifteen songs in one day, and four hundred in four days, is the largest amount of practicing I ever did.

Today [1900] my musical deafness is disappearing, and by sitting down to a piano and playing the lead notes, I can learn a song in less than one-tenth the time required when I first commenced to practice. (*Gospel Standards*, p. 354.)

Fourth, we must bolster our will or desire by riveting our minds upon the virtues of the desired habit. A person does not lick the smoking habit by relishing the pleasure of a cigarette. But rather, he or she gains resolve by thinking about the added health and vitality and savings he or she will realize when free of the habit. Motivation to lose weight comes by anticipating the increased good looks and vitality, not by savoring caloric foods and exotic dishes.

In the scriptures, we read of good desires and wills. Alma taught: "I know that [God] granteth unto men according to their desire, . . . yea, I know that he allotteth unto men . . . according to their wills" (Alma 29:4).

So, when you have made your resolve, build your case and build your will. Gather information, identify reasons, and do whatever you can to justify your struggle in acquiring the new habit.

Fifth, we must not look back or permit exceptions to occur once we have embarked upon our new course of action. No exceptions! Famous last words for the alcoholic are: "Just one more sip. I'll drink only this one, and then it's back on the wagon." Can't you just hear Lot's wife saying, as they raced away from Sodom, "Hold up for a minute; let me take one more look at the city." That was a fatal and very salty mistake (see Genesis 19:15–26).

Once we have determined the new habit or the improved pattern of living, we must guard against any inclination to deviate. No exceptions must be tolerated and no excuses invented. Every breach of our new resolution returns us to point zero, or below, and adds strength to the behavior we are trying to conquer.

"Look not behind thee" (Genesis 19:17) were the Lord's words to Lot and his company, and those words apply to you and to me as we seek to improve our lot.

Sixth, we must plunge wholeheartedly into the new program of conduct. Wholeheartedly: we must not let go of old habits gradually and move into new ones slowly. We must not taper off from the old, because that only prolongs the struggle. It also provides opportunities for the old habit to increase its hold. The new habit, if it is to survive, must be favored in every possible way and repeated in its complete form as often as possible.

I have suggested six steps to help cultivate new habits. Let me review the process quickly: (1) Define the desired habit, (2) bind yourself to act, (3) put the new conduct into operation, (4) bolster your will or desire, (5) do not look back, and (6) plunge wholeheartedly into the new conduct.

One Small Step at a Time

As you follow these steps, please bear in mind the need to take one resolve at a time. The big problem with most of our New Year's resolutions is that the list is generally too long and too ambitious. Our tendency to forsake our resolves seems to increase as the list grows. I believe that one resolve made and kept is better than a dozen made and abandoned. Therefore, move forward in your progress one step, one habit at a time.

I like the words of Hubbard: "It may not be out of place to say that every man (and woman) is controlled by Habit. When Habits are young they are like lion cubs, easily managed, but later there comes a time when they manage you. Bad Habits may put you on the Avernus Jerkwater, No. 23, with a ticket one way to Nowhere. Good Habits are mentors, guardian angels, and servants that regulate your sleep, your work, your thought" (*Selected Writings of Elbert Hubbard* [New York: William H. Wise, 1922] 2:195).

Sin — Brother of Bad Habits

Sin is the older and uglier brother of bad habit. Sin, like habit, can enter our lives in a seemingly innocuous way. It can begin small and occupy only a corner of our lives. Yet, if left unattended, countenanced, and allowed to flourish, it can consume our souls.

An ancient American prophet understood perfectly this concept of which I speak. He referred to the devil as the founder of sin and works of darkness and warned: "He [the devil] leadeth them by the neck with a flaxen cord, until he bindeth them with his strong cords forever" (2 Nephi 26:22).

Those who become followers of the evil one do not generally reach their captive state with one misdeed; they lose their freedom one sin at a time — one error after another — until almost all is lost. Flaxen cords are transformed into awful chains of steel as they allow themselves to follow the downward course. Each easy step away from the line of goodness and truth makes it more and more difficult to recover.

Several years ago, in a large city, my wife and I saw a sign in front of a church with this notice on the bulletin board: "Sunday Sermon Topic: Nice Sins for Good People." Though I did not attend these services, I have wondered ever since about the flattering and the pacifying and the lulling and the ear tickling that may have taken place in that setting.

Do not be deceived! There are no niceties, no goodnesses associated with sin, however small or large the transgression may appear. King David's flaxen-thread glance at Bathsheba resulted in the strong cords of adultery and death. The little murmurs of Laman and Lemuel led to the large breakup of a family and the splitting of a nation. Moreover, the little errors you and I commit can become very binding if not checked. It is written, "His own iniquities shall take the wicked himself, and he shall be holden with the cords of his sins" (Proverbs 5:22).

All of us from time to time need to make a careful assessment of our lives and determine our own state of affairs. And, if we find that we are encumbered with so-called "nice" sins or that we are a little reckless with goodness and truth, we must change. There is immediate danger in the little flaxen threads about us.

Repentance — Cultivating Good Habits

I would also suggest that the process of repentance is the means of escape from the clutches of sin and is not unlike the process of cultivating a desirable habit. Permit me to make the comparison:

Step one in habit formation, I said, was to define the habit. Equivalent action in repentance is recognition of error.

Step two in habit formation is to bind ourselves to action. This step in repentance is the resolve to do better.

Step three in habit formation is to put the new conduct into operation. In repenting, we reform our living pattern.

Step four in habit formation is to bolster will or desire. In repenting, we reflect seriously upon the forgiving nature of God and Christ's atonement.

Step five in habit formation is to not look back. In repentance, we refrain from committing the error again.

Step six in habit formation is to plunge wholeheartedly into the new conduct. This action in repentance is complete faith and reliance in the new direction we are taking.

Elder Bruce R. McConkie describes repentance as "the process whereby a mortal soul — unclean and stained with the guilt of sin—is enabled to cast off the burden of guilt, wash away the filth of iniquity, and become clean every whit, entirely free from the bondage of sin" (*Mormon Doctrine*, 2nd ed. [Salt Lake City: Bookcraft, 1966], p. 630).

Without the hopes and prospects embodied in the principle of repentance, perhaps many of us would be unable to retain our balance and sanity. We do err frequently; we do fall short of the mark; we often disappoint ourselves and those around us. If a means of escape and relief through repentance were not extended us, we would probably not be strong enough to cope with life. One sagging spirit, fettered by remorse for sin, cried out:

> *I wish that there were some wonderful place*
> *Called the Land of Beginning Again,*
> *Where all our mistakes and all our heartaches*
> *And all of our poor selfish grief*
> *Could be dropped like a shabby old coat at the door,*
> *And never be put on again.*
> (Louisa Fletcher, "The Land of Beginning Again," *Best Loved Poems of the American People*, selected by Hazel Felleman [New York: Doubleday, 1936], p. 101.)

How blessed we are to know that there is a "Land of Beginning Again"! This land is the gospel of Jesus Christ, and the door to it is that blessed principle of repentance. When we apply this principle in the Lord's way, cords and chains are removed, and we are freed from the enemies of our souls.

A Bad Beginning Is Not the End

Some years ago, Elder Robert L. Simpson, spoke about new beginnings and the principle of repentance. I would like to share with you just a portion of his inspired message. He said:

I can almost hear some of you saying at this very moment, "It's all so futile. Here I am only [38 days into the new year], and already I've goofed twice."

Young people, I want to assure you that you're not too far from par for the course. Just about everybody has had a bad start sometime or another. As I was watching the Rose Bowl game on television the other day, I had a flashback of something that happened on a high school football field not too far from that Rose Bowl many years ago when I was playing high school football. Speaking of getting off to a bad start, I think I hold the record. It was my first year of high school football. I'd been playing second string all through the practice games, and this was the first big league game. Six thousand cheering people were in the stands. As we were breaking after our halftime pep talk, the coach suddenly said, "Simpson, you start the second half." The old adrenaline came rushing, and I went charging out onto the field. This was my chance. Just about that time the coach said, "Oh, and by the way, I want you to kick off, Simpson." I determined right then and there that I was going to kick that ball farther than any football had ever been kicked in history. I really wanted to make a good showing on my first chance on the first string. Well, the referee waved his arm and blew his whistle. I could hear those six thousand people. I looked at that ball and came charging down the field. I felt everything tingling in my body; the excitement was so high. Well, you have probably already guessed it. I missed the ball. . . . But that isn't the half of it. This was back in the days when the quarterback held the ball with his finger. I broke the quarterback's finger.

Now, if you think that you're off to a bad start, I just want to set your mind at ease and let you know that it could be worse. I also want you to know that I had a coach that had confidence [in me] because he left me in. I don't know why, but he did, and I played the rest of the game. If I weren't so modest, I might also tell you that I made all-league that year. ("Your 1975 Game Plan,"

Speeches of the Year: BYU Centennial, Devotional, and Fireside Addresses, 1975 [Provo, Utah: BYU Press, 1976], pp. 319–20; also *Ensign,* January 1977, p. 83.]

I love the lesson that is taught in Elder Simpson's experience. A young man of less determination might have been bound to failure by missing that ball. And, if not by that, certainly by breaking the quarterback's finger. However, Elder Simpson had "plasticity" and confidence and resolve, and he repented of his error and made all-league.

Avoid the Chains of Satan

As you give further thought to what I have said about bad habits and sin, I hope you will retain foremost in your mind a scene that Enoch was privileged to see. He saw in his vision the coming of the Son of Man, the restoration of the gospel, and many other things. Then he heard a voice saying, "Wo, wo be unto the inhabitants of the earth." Then Enoch "beheld Satan; and he had a great chain in his hand, and it veiled the whole face of the earth with darkness; and he looked up and laughed, and his angels rejoiced" (Moses 7:25–26).

The chain held by Satan is referred to in the scriptures as "the chains of hell" (Alma 12:11), "the bands of iniquity" (Mosiah 23:12), "chains of darkness (2 Peter 2:4), and "the everlasting chains of death" (Alma 36:18). Such chains are used to make us captives of the evil one. Normally, they are not thrown over us suddenly or in one single act. They start as flaxen threads and encumber us habit by habit, sin by sin, and strand by strand. And if not cut and cast off through the process of repentance, they can become heavy chains and the awful "snare of the devil" (2 Timothy 2:26).

So, be very careful. As you serve the Lord, identify your weaknesses, replace bad habits with good ones, and avoid any and every appearance of evil. I have one desire for you, and that desire is that you will succeed in your calling. Please be careful. Do not allow the chains of Satan to fall upon you. Do not allow those little threads to encircle you about. Throw them off. Cut them loose. Do not allow Satan to make you his. Satan is uncomfortable, he is miserable, and he seeks to make us miserable like himself.

God bless you. I have perfect confidence in you and your ability to achieve success. I know that you can fill your calling honorably and develop the character that will help you to do so.

Chapter Eight

Serving as the Salt of the Earth

You and others called to serve in the the Church have been referred to as the salt of the earth. Such reference is very appropriate but at the same time very challenging. I say this because the word *savor* is related to how you live, and the word *savior* is related to how you serve.

Salt, as you know, contains two elements — sodium and chlorine — and is known chemically as sodium chloride. This white substance occupies an important place in our lives. It is essential to health; body cells must have salt in order to live and work. It has antiseptic, or germ-killing, properties. It is a preservative. It is an ingredient in many foods and products. In fact, it is estimated that salt has more than fourteen thousand uses.

According to the historians, "salt at one time had religious significance, and was a symbol of purity. . . . Among many peoples, salt is still used as a sign of honor, friendship, and hospitality. The Arabs say 'there is salt between us,' meaning 'we have eaten together, and are friends' " (*World Book Encyclopedia*, 1978, 17:69).

The Organizer and Creator of this world understood perfectly the nature and importance of salt. More than thirty-five references to this substance are found in the scriptures. In the Old Testament, mention is made of a "covenant of salt" (see Leviticus 2:13; Numbers 18:19; 2 Chronicles 13:5). In the New Testament, the Savior referred to his disciples as the "salt of the earth" and charged them to retain their savor (Matthew 5:13). He repeated this charge to his chosen disciples on the American continent: "I give unto you to be the salt of the earth; but if the salt shall lose its savor wherewith shall the earth be salted? The salt shall be thenceforth good for nothing, but to be cast out and to be trodden under foot of men" (3 Nephi 12:13).

How many times have we read, or heard others read, this scripture? Yet, do we understand fully the "salt of the earth" message? Are we conversant with the analogy? Are we responding properly to its implications?

Permit me to explain the savor and savior roles we have been called to fulfill as members of the Church and as the salt of the modern world.

The Savor of Men

In 1833, Joseph Smith received a revelation that included these instructions: "When men are called into mine everlasting gospel, and covenant with an everlasting covenant, they are accounted as the salt of the earth and the savor of men; they are called to be the savor of men" (D&C 101:39–40).

The word savor denotes taste, pleasing flavor, interesting quality, and high repute. Some salt has savor. That is, it is clean, pure, uncontaminated, and useful. In this state or condition, salt will preserve, flavor, heal, and perform other useful functions. Other salt is said to have lost its savor. It has lost its savor because it has been mixed with things of bad taste. In fact, it has taken on some of the color and appearance of other substances.

When the Lord used the expression "savor of men," he was speaking of those who represent him. He was referring to those who have repented, who have been washed clean in the waters of baptism, and who have covenanted to take upon them his name and his cause. Moreover, he was speaking of those who would share by covenant his priesthood power. He was speaking of you and me.

A world-renowned chemist told me that salt will not lose its savor with age. Savor is lost through mixture and contamination. Similarly, the power of testimony and service does not dissipate with age; it, too, is lost through mixture and contamination.

If we mix our thoughts with pornographic literature, we suffer a loss of savor.

If we mix our speech with lies or profanity, we suffer a loss of savor.

If we follow the crowd and become involved in immoral acts and the use of drugs, tobacco, alcohol, and other injurious substances, we lose savor.

Flavor and quality flee us if we contaminate our minds with unclean thoughts, desecrate our mouths by speaking less than the truth, and misapply our strength in performing evil acts. King Benjamin cautioned, "Watch yourselves, and your thoughts, and your words, and your deeds, and observe the commandments of God" (Mosiah 4:30).

I would offer these simple guidelines as the means to preserve our savor: If it is not clean, do not think it; if it is not true, do not speak it; if it is not good, do not do it (see Marcus Aurelius, "The Meditations of Marcus Aurelius," in *The Harvard Classics*, Charles W. Eliot, ed. [New York: P. F. Collier and Son, 1909], p. 211).

Cleanliness, truth, and goodness have always been and will ever be the watchwords of those with savor. It is said that 65 percent or more of our communications are nonverbal. If this is so, who we are and what we are is most important. President Spencer W. Kimball declared, "No greater service can be given to [a] . . . calling of the Church than to exemplify positive Christian virtues in our lives" (*Ensign*, November 1978, p. 6).

We must fight daily to retain our savor, our purity. We must press forward, clinging to our standards of holiness, remembering all the while that we are called to be the savor of men.

Saviors of Men

The Prophet Joseph Smith received these instructions from the Lord: "They were set to be a light unto the world, and to be the saviors of men; and inasmuch as they are not the saviors of men, they are as salt that has lost its savor" (D&C 103:9–10).

One of the grandest concepts in the gospel of Jesus Christ is the concept that we can and should be more than passive observers in the cause of saving souls. One Church leader taught: "In our preexistent state . . . we made a certain agreement with the Almighty. . . . We agreed . . . to be not only saviors for ourselves but measurably, saviors for the whole human family. We went into a partnership with the Lord. The working out of the plan became then not merely the Father's work, and the Savior's work, but also our work" (John A. Widtsoe, *Utah Genealogical and Historical Magazine*, October 1934, p. 189).

I know of a young priest who was asked by his bishop to fellowship an inactive quorum member. The bishop said that others had failed in their attempts to recover the boy. The final words of the bishop's commission were: "Please save him." After many tries and failures, the miracle was wrought—the inactive returned to full activity in the quorum. It was thrilling for me to hear the hero in this experience bear testimony of the joy he had received as a result of his soul-saving efforts.

A short time ago, two missionaries visited a widow who had expressed interest in the Church. She was ill and had been advised by her physician that a kidney was to be removed. The elders comforted the woman, heeded the whisperings of the Spirit, and pronounced a blessing. Another miracle happened. The operation was canceled, and the missionaries began teaching their friend the gospel. A baptismal date was set. This particular woman will never forget the blessing and teachings of the elders. She will hold them in cherished memory and regard them as "saviors of men."

One brother tells of how he was guided by the Spirit in locating thousands of names on one of his father's ancestral lines. When the necessary research was completed, he and his wife and others completed the appropriate temple ordinances. In summarizing his experience, he said: "It taught me that if a person will put forth the effort to search, the way will be opened up and he will obtain the spirit of Elijah. . . . I firmly believe that in the preexistence we made a commitment . . . to be a savior to these people, doing all the necessary research and having the temple work done for them" (Jared Suess, "Twice Rescued," in *Links of Forever*, comp. Connie Rector and Diane Deputy [Salt Lake City: Bookcraft, 1977], p. 120).

Concluding Thoughts

There should be salt between us and all people. We should extend honor, friendship, and hospitality to all of our brothers and sisters. To the inactives we extend the hand of fellowship; to the nonmembers we extend the divine invitation "come and see"; with our ancestors we establish sacred links welding parents to children and children to parents. In all of this, we advance the purposes of the Master and assist in the reconciliation of mortals to the God who gave them life. And, in the process, we not only preserve our savor but also we save ourselves.

I count it significant that the headquarters of The Church of Jesus Christ of Latter-day Saints is located in *Salt Lake City.* From this center of the Church flows the message of salvation to all the world. To this city of salt, men and women gather from all corners of the earth to receive instruction and edification. Such instruction, if accepted and practiced, will enable them to retain their savor and help them become saviors of men.

I pray that you and all who serve in the Church will appreciate more perfectly the words of the Savior: "Ye are the salt of the earth." May you carry this designation faithfully and honorably.

Please remember that people — like salt — lose their savor through contamination; remember also that those who fail to use their talents in behalf of others are like salt without savor.

I testify that an abiding and exalting relationship with the Master is established as we live to be pure in savor and to be saviors of our fellow beings. This I declare, adding my witness that the Master lives and directs his church today.

Chapter Nine

Establishing Synergistic Relationships

When people receive callings in the Church, they often find themselves working closely with people who are quite different from themselves, even people they might not ordinarily seek out as friends. This is undoubtedly exactly what the Lord intends, and it presents some interesting challenges and marvelous opportunities.

Two Worlds Meet

When I reported to the mission home in Salt Lake City many years ago, I was introduced to a tall, frail, scholarly looking young man. I quickly sized him up and decided that my associate was a spoiled city boy from the East. I determined immediately that we were a terrible mismatch, and I wondered just how long I could endure the ordeal of eating, sleeping, working, and worshipping with my strange companion.

It took us several days to travel via train to New York

City. I thought the trip would never end! Not once did my companion mention basketball, football, baseball, tennis, track, and the other "basics" of life. Instead, he talked incessantly about music, his mother, and other suspect subjects. To add insult to injury, when we were to leave New York City for our field of labor, our ship became involved in a port-of-entry dispute and was detained in New York Harbor for an extra week. That week seemed like an eternity!

During the first few days on the water, both seasickness and the thrill of sailing on an ocean liner took my mind off my predicament. But this diversion of attention was short-lived. Soon the monotony of the three-week voyage caused me to notice more faults in my companion. I learned that he had a nervous habit of grinding his teeth in his sleep. (I rudely pointed out this peculiarity to my companion, but he didn't believe me because he couldn't duplicate this hideous sound while conscious.) He brushed his teeth mechanically fifty times up, fifty times down, and fifty times sideways before and after each meal. He chewed each mouthful of food twenty-five times faithfully before swallowing; this I know to be a fact because I counted.

A Violent Clash

At last we reached our mission field and were assigned a proselyting area. My expectations for a reprieve, however, vanished when I learned that we were the only two missionaries in that field of labor. I was trapped! All thoughts of a transfer to another elder were painfully junked, and I embarked grudgingly in the adjustment to mission life. The days wore on—grindingly.

Although I became busily engaged in learning a new language and in developing teaching skills, I took time to note that my companion had a strange walking gait. It bothered me to no end that his strides were not synchronized with mine. He had a strange way of wearing his hat and tying his tie — this also bothered me. He didn't like Wheaties. He sang while he did dishes. And to top it all off, he always had something significant to say. The fact that he was also a superior student of the language and the gospel created even greater resentment.

Needless to say, the missionary work did not flourish in this atmosphere of contention. Door receptions were generally hostile. People were not interested in our message. The spirit for proselyting was lacking. Prayers seemed vacant, and all efforts to teach appeared futile.

Finally, one day while tracting, the whole matter came to a climax. It was my turn to give the approach. I did so, and my listener slammed the door in my face. This pleased my companion, and he started to snicker. I burned inside, just waiting for my opportunity to retaliate. At the next door, my companion gave the approach. His reception was as cold as mine had been, so I laughed. My offended companion looked at me with disgust and said: "Let's go home. How can we preach the gospel of love when there is no love or understanding between us?" I agreed.

An Unveiling

When we reached our apartment, my companion sat on one side of the room and I sat on the other. After an awkward silence, he said, "I know you don't like me, so why don't you tell me all the things about me that you despise." This was the opportunity for which I had been waiting. I began a long dissertation about grinding teeth, music, eating habits, and so on, which lasted for several minutes. My attack was brutal! When I had finished my critical review, my companion said that he was going to cite some of my weaknesses. I supported the proposal, feeling confident that he could not possibly have more than one or two things to say.

For the next half hour, I sat in stunned silence as my companion delineated my long list of faults. I could hardly believe what I heard. My distorted self-image was exposed, judged, and crucified in one fell swoop. What a clod I had been!

Finally, when the exchange of criticisms was ended, my companion looked at me and I looked at him, and we were both ashamed. We were ashamed of our puffed-up pride, our selfishness, our narrow vision, and our self-centered ways of living. We knew full well that we had erred in permitting petty differences to block out the missionary spirit. A recognition of our hypocritical introduction to missionary work troubled our consciences. Both of us were sorry about our past actions and were anxious to repent.

A New Beginning

With broken hearts and contrite spirits, we knelt together and prayed for forgiveness. My companion prayed first, and then I followed. Each of us acknowledged his shortcomings before the Lord and begged for forgiveness. Both of us pleaded for strength in overcoming selfishness, pride, and the other barriers that had severed communications and strained our relationship. I don't remember how long we prayed. I do know that it was long enough for the tears to wash my face and stain the bedspread.

Upon finishing our petition for divine cleansing, we stood and looked at each other. I slowly extended my hand to my companion, asked for his forgiveness, and pledged that I would do whatever was necessary to regain his trust and to create the proper missionary companionship. I even promised that I would try to share his interest in music. My companion made a similar resolve. Included in his pledge was the agreement that he would spend a portion of his preparation day throwing a silly little ball through a hoop stationed at the end of a clay court. For the first time in our stormy association, the static was clear from our receivers, and heart-to-heart communication occurred.

David and Jonathan

I don't recall exactly how long my companion and I were together. In time, more missionaries did come to our area, and we were assigned other companions. I do know that a considerable portion of my time in the mission field was spent laboring with this unforgettable young man.

Once we had reached an understanding and had included charity (the pure love of Christ) in our twosome, we couldn't get enough of each other. Our friendship assumed a special character and has continued to this day. This elder is my brother. He is a special friend—one I shall never be able to repay for all he has given me. How can one pay another for polishing personality, refining character, and instilling an abiding love of the gospel?

Though our beginnings were difficult, eventually, as with David and Jonathan of old, "the soul of [Carlos] was knit with the soul of [his companion], and [Carlos] loved him as his own soul" (see 1 Samuel 18:1).

Synergism

Synergism, it is said, is an old Christian doctrine. It purports that the grace of God combined with the good works of mortals results in full salvation.

In our time, synergism is defined as "the simultaneous action of separate agencies which, together, have greater total effect than the sum of their individual effects" (*Webster's New World Dictionary*, p. 1444).

This principle may be illustrated as follows:

A 2×4 eight feet long, standing on end, can bear a weight of 615 pounds. If a second 2×4 eight feet long is nailed to the first, together they can bear not 1,230 pounds (double 615 pounds) but rather 2,400 pounds.

A 2 × 6 beam ten feet long, I am told, can bear 400 pounds. If a second 2 × 6 beam is nailed to the first, the strength of the two beams is quadrupled to 1,600 pounds!

In both these instances, two are not simply twice as strong as one. Two are four times as strong as one! This is synergism.

Synergism in the Ancient Church

God, the master architect and engineer of the universe, knows and applies all laws perfectly. He knows the limited strength of one board as opposed to two. He also knows the limited strength of one person as opposed to two or three or more. In the meridian of time, he called twelve men as his special witnesses, his apostles. Others, referred to as seventies, he also called. Eventually he called Peter, James, and John to serve together as the First Presidency of his church.

The Lord's representatives in ancient times (Peter, James, John, Paul, and all the rest) were given power over unclean spirits. This power had its roots in the priesthood that had been conferred upon them. However, they received added power from the special commission given them and the synergistic companionship to which they were assigned.

I thrill when I read of Paul and Barnabas at Lystra. So powerful were these two — as one complemented the other — that the people said, "The gods are come down to us in the likeness of men" (Acts 14:11). Paul they called Mercurius; Barnabas they called Jupiter.

Synergism in the Church Today

Soon after the gospel was restored, the Prophet Joseph Smith received instructions about the missionary work that was to be launched worldwide. Included in these instructions were these words: "Ye shall go forth in the power of my Spirit, preaching my gospel, two by two, in my name, lifting up your voices as with the sound of a trump, declaring my word like unto angels of God" (D&C 42:6).

Reasons for serving with others are many and quite apparent. They include the following:

1. *The need for two or more witnesses.* The Lord has declared more than once, "In the mouth of two or three witnesses shall every word be established" (2 Corinthians 13:1; see also Deuteronomy 17:6; Matthew 18:16; Ether 5:4; D&C 6:28, 128:3). People serving together teach and bear witness of the work they share. Each testifies of what the other says. Moreover, each witnesses in behalf of the other, refuting the words of false accusers or others who would defile the truth.

2. *Support in teaching.* Alma and Amulek constituted a powerful companionship. According to the account in the Book of Mormon, "[Alma] began to speak . . . and to establish the words of Amulek, and to explain things beyond, or to unfold the scriptures beyond that which Amulek had done" (Alma 12:1). Two minds are, generally speaking, better than one. When both are concentrated upon the same task or purpose, mutual support may be enjoyed.

3. *Protection.* The preacher said: "Two are better than one; because they have a good reward for their labor. For if they fall, the one will lift up his fellow: but woe to him that is alone when he falleth; for he hath not another to help him up . . . and if one prevail against him, two shall withstand him" (Ecclesiastes 4:9–10, 12).

4. *Strengthen one another.* There are many scriptures that explain the need to strengthen those with whom we serve. I shall cite only four:

The Lord said, Simon, Simon, behold, Satan hath desired to have you, that he may sift you as wheat: But I have prayed for thee, that thy faith fail not: and when thou art converted, *strengthen thy brethren* (Luke 22:31–32; italics added).

If any man among you be strong in the Spirit, let him take with him him that is weak, that he may be edified in all meekness, *that he may become strong also* (D&C 84:106; italics added).

We then that are strong [experienced] ought to bear the infirmities of the weak [inexperienced], and not to please ourselves. Let every one of us please his [companion] for his good to edification (Romans 15:1–2).

Strengthen your brethren in all your conversation, in all your prayers, in all your exhortations, and in all your doings (D&C 108:7).

5. *Counsel.* One of the greatest benefits of serving with others relates to counsel. Those older or more experienced share what they have learned; those younger or less experienced provide fresh insights and new enthusiasm. All have something valuable to contribute.

Alma counseled one of his sons: "I command you to take it upon you to counsel with your elder brothers in your undertakings; for behold, thou art in thy youth, and ye stand in need to be nourished by your brothers. And give heed to their counsel" (Alma 39:10; see also 1 Peter 5:5).

These are only five of the benefits of serving with others. Other and related reasons could be listed. Please understand that synergistic powers are unleashed as servants of the Lord witness, support, protect, strengthen, and counsel one another.

Developing Sustaining Relationships

There are many factors involved in developing sustaining relationships. Such relationships do not evolve overnight, nor do they occur spontaneously. They require earnest effort, and they must be worked for. Below are some suggestions on how this might be done:

1. *Have empathy.* In 586 B.C., Ezekiel became angry with his people because they forgot God and turned to the worship of idols. Filled with righteous indignation, he intended to deal with them harshly. However, he proceeded to the river Chebar and "sat where they sat, and remained there astonished among them seven days" (Ezekiel 3:15). This experience changed his perception of things and caused him to preach with more compassion.

The need for empathy is suggested in a prayer spoken by the Sioux Indians: "Great Spirit, help me never to judge another until I have walked for two weeks in his moccasins."

2. *Promote open communication.* One Church leader said: "In an atmosphere of sincere love . . . communication is pleasant, and adjustment is easy. But when this relation is impaired and one lives primarily for his own likes and self-interest, communication fails and real difficulties arise." Amos asked, "Can two walk together, except they be agreed?" (Amos 3:3).

Few actions canker a relationship faster than no words or actions at all. There must be open and building conversation between those who serve together.

3. *Look for reflections.* Someone remarked facetiously to his wife: "Everyone is a little strange except for thee and me, and even thou art a little strange." There is a truism that we see what we want to see. Too many times, we view in the mirror a reflection of what we want to see and not what actually is. Perhaps we should seek to obtain a clear view of ourselves as reflected through the eyes of a close companion. Remember the words of the Savior: "Why beholdest thou the mote that is in thy brother's eye, but con-

siderest not the beam that is in thine own eye?" (Matthew 7:3).

4. *Extend service.* King Benjamin counseled parents to teach their children "to love one another, and to serve one another" (Mosiah 4:15). The two—love and service—go together. People who extend acts of kindness to one another will feel a bond of love and respect growing between them. And, eventually, they will create that oneness that should typify the relationship between servants of God (see D&C 38:27; 1 Corinthians 1:10).

5. *Study and pray together.* I know of nothing more welding to a relationship than studying the gospel and praying together. The gospel is a binding thread that knits heart to heart and soul to soul. And prayer brings yet another party, God, into the association and clinches the supportive arrangement.

6. *Find joy in the success of others.* Said Alma: "I do not joy in my own success alone, but my joy is more full because of the success of my brethren. . . . Behold, they have labored exceedingly, and have brought forth much fruit; and how great shall be their reward! . . . When I think of the success of these my brethren . . . great is my joy" (Alma 29:14–16).

Look for the good in others and learn. Give sincere credit where credit is due. Spend less time fault-finding and more time identifying strengths. Yes, try to catch others doing good! Don't put a stumbling block before others; instead, give them a step upward in the form of a recognized success (see Romans 14:13).

7. *Correct in love.* If correction is necessary, it should be made in love and in the spirit of helpfulness. It must be done gently and with love unfeigned. Moreover, it must include an increase of love afterward (see D&C 121:41–46).

We must realize that we are our brothers' and sisters'

keepers, and that we share responsibility for the welfare of others.

Conclusion

Some time ago, I heard a missionary confess, "My companion and I don't get along very well. We are working on a 50 percent or less performance level. We could double our production if we were united and pulling together."

It is sad when such a relationship exists between servants of the Lord Jesus Christ. What a waste of time and resources! How contrary to the spirit and calling of a Church representative!

More than one mission has adopted the following motto: "Me lift thee and thee lift me, and we will both ascend together" (Whittier).

I like these words because they conform with this divine teaching: "If a man say, I love God, and hateth his brother, he is a liar: for he that loveth not his brother whom he hath seen, how can he love God whom he hath not seen? And this commandment have we from him, that he who loveth God love his brother also" (1 John 4:20–21).

God bless you and all of his servants to form sanctifying relationships so that synergistic powers may be rallied in behalf of the restored gospel and the kingdom of God on earth.

Chapter Ten

Making the Most
of Opportunities

At some point during your Church service, you will begin to wonder when you might be released. You will look behind you and be surprised at how much time has gone by since you were set apart. Time does fly on wings of lightning, just as the song suggests, and we wonder where it has gone (see "Improve the Shining Moments," *Hymns of The Church of Jesus Christ of Latter-day Saints* [Salt Lake City: The Church of Jesus Christ of Latter-day Saints, 1985], no. 226). You may also be concerned about whether or not you are making the most of your opportunities in your calling. I would be disappointed if you didn't harbor such feelings. I hope you will always regard your work as being urgent and your opportunities to serve as being very precious; otherwise, you might become complacent and easily satisfied by a mediocre performance. I have heard it said that we all tend to do better when we run a little scared or wonder whether we are doing all that we should be doing.

I once knew a missionary who was always "a fix'n" to do his duty but who never really ever got started. I knew another one who was always anticipating a new companion or the next transfer, supposing that a change of circumstances would help him get launched. A third one seemed to have a difficult time understanding just what he was expected to do. All three of these cases were out of the ordinary; however, they served to remind me and others of the damning consequences of procrastinating time, "looking beyond the mark," and living without a purpose. And, because all of us at times show tinges of these stifling tendencies, perhaps we should give them some thoughtful consideration.

Three Questions

Russian author Leo Tolstoi wrote a provocative short story entitled "The Three Questions." The story begins as follows:

> It once occurred to a certain king that if he always knew the right time to begin everything; if he knew who were the right people to listen to, and whom to avoid; and, above all, if he always knew what was the most important thing to do, he would never fail in anything he might undertake.
>
> And this thought having occurred to him, he had it proclaimed throughout his kingdom that he would give a great reward to any one who would teach him what was the right time for every action, and who were the most necessary people, and how he might know what was the most important thing to do (In *The Works of Leo Tolstoi* [New York: Black's Readers Service Co., 1928], p. 23).

Many learned people came to the king and attempted to answer his questions. The answers to the three questions were varied and thought-provoking, but none were fully acceptable.

Later, the king heard of a hermit known widely for his wisdom. The hermit lived a secluded life deep in the forest, so the king went to him. And, after some interesting events well worth the reading, wherein the king helps to save the life of an enemy, the story concludes with these words:

> "Do you not see," replied the hermit. "If you had not pitied my weakness yesterday, and had not dug those beds for me, but had gone your way, that man would have attacked you, and you would have repented of not having stayed with me. So the most important time was when you were digging the beds; and I was the most important man; and to do me good was your most important business. Afterwards when that man ran to us, the most important time was when you were attending to him, for if you had not bound up his wounds he would have died without having made peace with you. So he was the most important man, and what you did for him was your most important business.
>
> "Remember then: there is only one time that is important—now! It is the most important time because it is the only time when we have any power. The most necessary man is he with whom you are, for no man knows whether he will ever have dealings with anyone else; and the most important affair is, to do him good, because for that purpose alone was man sent into this life!" (Ibid., p. 25.)

The Right Time

The older one grows, the more one recognizes that there is an eternal rhythm to life. In the words of the poet, "there is a season, and a time to every purpose under the heaven: a time to be born, and a time to die; a time to plant, and a time to [harvest]" (Ecclesiastes 3:1–2). Our task is to obey that rhythm and to make the most of the time allotted us.

A calling is life in miniature. It, too, has a beginning and an end, with much planting and harvesting in between. The beginning is the issuance of a call; the end is the extension of a release; and, the intervening period is the right time for us to perform our labors. A calling, much like life itself, is "a probationary time, a time to repent and serve God" (Alma 42:4).

Those who live and serve with their eyes upon the past allow the world to pass them by. Those who live and serve with their eyes upon the prospects of the future are often blind to the opportunities of the present. But, those who live and serve in day-tight compartments, squeezing the most from each twenty-four hour period, will escape the monster called procrastination and gain the most from their experience.

Amulek taught, "The day of this life [or calling] is the day for men to perform their labors." Then he warned, "If we do not *improve* our time while in this life [calling], then cometh the night of darkness [or release] wherein there can be no labor performed" (Alma 34:32–33; italics added).

I find inspiration and wisdom in the hymn "oi5 the Shining Moments." It constitutes a sermon that a calling in the Church is "quick in passing" and is "as a single day" when viewed from an eternal perspective. Ponder these words:

> *Improve the shining moments;*
> *Don't let them pass you by.*
> *Work while the sun is radiant;*
> *Work, for the night draws nigh.*
> *We cannot bid the sunbeams*
> *To lengthen out their stay,*
> *Nor can we ask the shadow*
> *To ever stay away.*
>
> *Time flies on wings of lightning;*

We cannot call it back.
It comes, then passes forward
Along its onward track.
And if we are not mindful,
The chance will fade away,
For life is quick in passing.
'Tis as a single day.

As wintertime doth follow
The pleasant summer days,
So may our joys all vanish
And pass far from our gaze.
Then should we not endeavor
Each day some point to gain,
That we may here be useful
And ev'ry wrong disdain?

Improve each shining moment.
In this you are secure,
For promptness bringeth safety
And blessings rich and pure.
Let prudence guide your actions;
Be honest in your heart;
And God will love and bless you
And help to you impart.
(Hymns, no. 226.)

I have heard of a missionary who was told in his setting apart that he would not return home. He concluded that one of two things would occur: (1) he would live and serve the rest of his life in his appointed mission field, or (2) he would die while serving his mission. It is reported that with these thoughts in mind, he served as if each day were his last. Whether the story is true or not, it is a lesson to all who have been called to serve God and who are expected to serve with all their "heart, might, mind, and strength" (D&C 4:2).

So, I urge you to remember that the right time is now!

You must consider today's time as one of your most precious assets and use it wisely. You will want to plan carefully your activities and schedule yourself accordingly, placing yourself as the master, and not the serf, of time. A calling in the Church comes and goes like a dream in the night and must not be misspent (see Jacob 7:26).

The Right People

The king in Tolstoi's account learned that the most necessary person is the person with whom you are. For, as the hermit explained, "no man knows whether he will ever have dealings with anyone else." This suggests that we must have a love and concern for those among whom we serve. We must not serve with an eye over our shoulder toward past activities or elsewhere. Our interests must be centered in our fellow servants, our leaders, those we serve, and God.

Laman and Lemuel were always looking and hearkening back to Jerusalem. Rather than listening to Nephi, Lehi, and God — the right people — they were concerned with the old days and the old people of a doomed society. It is sad that they failed to recognize their brother, "whose views [had] been glorious," as the most necessary person and the one to whom they should have listened (see 2 Nephi 1:24).

I almost weep in reading that the Jews rejected the prophets and Christ "because of their blindness, which blindness came by looking beyond the mark" (Jacob 4:14). They crucified the Savior — the most necessary person who ever walked the earth — and had dealings with the wrong people.

We must have faith that our callings are inspired and that the people with whom we work are important. This applies to our associates and, more especially, to the people we seek to serve.

The king in Tolstoi's story learned that the man whose wounds he bound and whose life he saved was the most important man. Such is the case with those who seek to heal people spiritually and to reconcile them with God. Each soul is of great worth and deserves our "here-and-now" attention.

I've heard converts say to missionaries, "God sent you to me" or "You were raised up to help this people." I like to think that there is more than a little truth in these statements. I say this because I know that calls and assignments are inspired and that the Lord knows how to match his servants and his fields of labor.

You must love the people among whom you work. Learn their needs; find out their concerns; regard them as children of God with inherent goodnesses. Moreover, when you serve them, view them in terms of what they can become. These actions will help you understand that the most necessary people — the right people — are those with whom you are, for you don't know whether you will ever have dealings with anyone else.

The Right Thing to Do

When the king in the story to which we have referred received answers to the third question from the sages in his kingdom, they cited many important occupations. Some said that science was the most important work in the world. Others said that skill in warfare took precedence over all of life's pursuits. A few felt that religious worship should come first.

The true answer to the question of what is the right thing to do is found in the scriptures. God said to John Whitmer and others: "The thing which will be of the most worth unto you will be to declare repentance unto this people, that you may bring souls unto me, that you may rest with them in the kingdom of my Father" (D&C 15:6).

How could any other work be rated or judged as more important than that of saving souls?

The openly avowed purpose of Deity is stated clearly: "This is my work and my glory—to bring to pass the immortality and eternal life of man" (Moses 1:39).

If this is Father's purpose, should it not also be our purpose and the focal point of all our doings? We are his children, and he does work through us to accomplish his holy work.

The Apostle Paul wrote: "It is good to be zealously affected always in a good thing" (Galations 4:18). In a modern revelation, the Lord adds: "Men should be anxiously engaged in a good cause, and do many things of their own free will, and bring to pass much righteousness; . . . and inasmuch as men do good they shall in nowise lose their reward" (D&C 58:27–28).

There is no work more right or more important than the work in which you are involved. Your commission is simple, to do good for others. You must, therefore, share the light and virtue that is in you and invite people to come unto Christ "and bring forth works of righteousness" (Alma 5:35).

In Conclusion

In summary, I repeat the concluding paragraph in Tolstoi's story of "The Three Questions": "Remember then: there is only one time that is important—now! It is the most important time because it is the only time when we have any power. The most necessary man is he with whom you are, for no man knows whether he will ever have dealings with anyone else; and the most important affair is, to do him good, because for that purpose alone was man sent into this life!" (*The Works of Leo Tolstoi*, p. 25).

My great desire and prayer is that you will make the most of your opportunities in your calling.

Chapter Eleven

Setting and Striving to Reach Goals

An important part of any calling in the Church is setting goals. Much is said about goals in the business world and in almost every field of human endeavor. Many motivational groups have been organized to market techniques pertaining to goal setting and goal striving. And, there is a tendency for some to regard goal setting as a panacea for all the problems relating to a person's performance of duty. But, like many other things, goal setting is really a process with various strengths and weaknesses that depend on how it is understood and applied.

There are some aspects of your calling over which you have full control. I refer to such things as how much time you spend studying the handbook, the hours you spend preparing for a class, the time you spend in interviews, and other personal and manageable activities. Therefore, establishing goals for such things seems to make real sense and comes rather naturally.

However, there are other aspects of your calling — such as the number of people who will believe what you teach them or follow counsel you give them — over which you do not have full control. People do have their agency and must not be forced in a satanic manner by servants of the Lord Jesus Christ. Consequently, you must do what you can to teach, counsel, and serve others, knowing all the while that the harvest will ultimately be determined by another source or power. As the Apostle Paul wrote, "I have planted, Apollos watered; but *God gave the increase*" (1 Corinthians 3:6; italics added). So, goal setting, as applied to these partially controlled aspects of your work, must be done carefully, wisely, and in full compliance with spiritual influences.

Set and Strive to Reach Goals

I have long contended that those who set goals are masters of their own fate. Contrariwise, those without goals become the pawn of time, circumstance, and every wind of influence. President Spencer W. Kimball had this in mind, I think, when he said, "I am convinced that unless we set goals, we move no place."

To me, goals give purpose and direction to life. Have you ever thought what might happen to the game of football if we removed the goal post and erased the goal line? How would we keep the score? How would we know whether we were winning or losing? How would we maintain interest among the players?

In my youth, I would refuse to play a game of basketball if someone suggested that we play for "funzies" and not keep score. What purpose does the game serve if we don't receive credit for putting that ball through the little hoop? How can we get excited or motivated about our involvement in something if we don't count and mark successful efforts?

Ward Cantrell said, "Apathy can be overcome by en-

thusiasm, and enthusiasm can be aroused by only two
things: (1) an ideal (or purpose) that takes the imagination
by storm; (2) a definite intelligible plan for carrying that
ideal into practice.''

Goals that are challenging and yet attainable do excite
the imagination and stir interest. Then, when a plan is
drafted for achieving those goals, strong anticipation is gen-
erated. The goals and the plan work together synergistically
in drawing performance upward.

A Divine Model

God, our Father, has an avowed purpose and goal. It is
"to bring to pass the immortality and eternal life of man"
(Moses 1:39). Moreover, he has a plan for the accomplishment of his goal. We refer to that plan as the plan of salvation
or the gospel of Jesus Christ (see Alma 42). Added to all of
that, note God's goal-striving determination in these scriptures:

> God doth not walk in crooked paths, neither doth he
> turn to the right hand nor to the left, neither doth he vary
> from that which he hath said, therefore his paths are
> straight, and his course is one eternal round (D&C 3:2).
>
> There is nothing that the Lord thy God shall take in
> his heart to do but what he will do it (Abraham 3:17).

If these are not firm declarations of intent and strong
resolve, I don't know what is.

The Apostle Paul described his goal striving in these
words: "This one thing I do, forgetting those things which
are behind, and reaching forth unto those things which are
before, I press toward the mark for the prize of the high
calling of God in Christ Jesus" (Philippians 3:13–14).

Words of Caution

Before I explain the goal-setting process I feel is appropriate in Church callings, permit me to voice some words of caution:

1. Impure motives or selfish desire must not be reflected in goals. One specialist in human behavior wrote: "Striving for goals which are important to you, not as status symbols, but because they are consistent with your own deep inner wants, is healthful. Striving for real success — for *your* success — through creative accomplishment, brings a deep inner satisfaction. Striving for a phony success to please others brings a phony satisfaction" (Maxwell Maltz, *Psycho-Cybernetics* [New York: Pocket Books, 1969], pp. 146–47).

I know of some people who have "padded" the record and pushed aside people and principles, all in the name of goal setting and goal striving. Such behavior leads to ultimate failure and hollow pseudo-successes. The motives undergirding our goals must be pure, and the actions directed toward achieving goals must be Christian and in full harmony with the spirit of the Lord's work.

2. Goals must not be too rigid or approached in a mechanistic manner. Overly rigid goals can, in certain circumstances, cause us to turn a deaf ear to the promptings of the Holy Spirit and to overlook spontaneous opportunities. I am not suggesting that a goal be of a "wishy-washy-watery" variety. This type is useless. But, I do feel that goals must be analyzed frequently and adjusted upward or downward occasionally in accord with inspiration received and changes of circumstances.

3. Goals must not be set as a means of forcing divine will or offending human agency. I know of a missionary who nearly lost his testimony because he and his companion failed to realize a baptismal goal of a certain number of people in a given month. He contended that they had prayed

about the number, felt good about it, presented it to the Lord, and received the Lord's confirmation. When they fell short of the mark, he blamed God for the shortfall.

We must not conclude that we can arbitrarily fix a number in our heads and automatically realize it. This is particularly true when we are dealing with spiritual matters and with people, who have their agency. To do so, I fear, under most circumstances, is to ask for "that which is contrary to [God's] will" (see Helaman 10:4–5; 2 Nephi 4:35).

Principles of Setting Goals

Though I have already alluded to some of the principles of goal setting, let me state six of prime significance:

1. Goals must be personal, not imposed by an outside source.
2. Goals must be challenging yet attainable.
3. Goals must be specific and clearly understood.
4. Goals should be verbalized for commitment purposes.
5. Goals should be visualized for motivational purposes.
6. Goals should be verified for monitoring purposes.

The Process of Setting Goals

There is a process to help in setting goals. The steps in the process are:

1. Obtain a vision — set a goal.
2. Obtain confirmation of the Spirit — seek inspiration.
3. Prepare a plan of action.
4. Work diligently to reach the objective.

As an example, I will apply the process to members and their personal scripture-study program. First, we sense the need to read the Book of Mormon. We know little about it and realize that we must become acquainted with this sacred volume of scripture. Coverage of the book is our major concern; in-depth study will come later.

Step 1: Obtain a vision—set a goal. Knowing that we have one hour of personal study a day, and knowing from past experience that we can read fifteen to twenty pages of scripture an hour, we determine that we can read the book from cover to cover in thirty days, if we push ourselves. So we write in our journal or planner our goal: "To read the Book of Mormon for coverage in thirty days: January 1–30." We also want to define a specific concept or teaching that we will search for to give our reading more purpose. We decide to find and underline all "Come unto Christ" references. Now we have a personal, challenging, and specific goal.

Step 2: Obtain confirmation of the Spirit—seek inspiration. We confirm our goal through study, prayer, and the spirit of revelation. We seek for the burning within our bosom, the whisperings within our mind and heart, and the peace of mind that comes when something is right and in accord with divine will (see D&C 9:8–9; 8:2–3; 6:22–24).

At the same time, we pray that our resolve will remain strong until the goal is reached. We pray that we will be inspired in our planning. And, we pray that our actions will bear fruit and prove acceptable to the Lord.

We receive added confirmation and inspiration as we share our declared purpose with others. Such verbalization of intent commits us even more to the goal and builds an expectancy of performance that is highly motivating. Those with whom the resolve is shared will help to "keep our feet to the fire" until the goal is achieved.

Step 3: Prepare a plan of action. In preparing a plan of action, we must draw upon all of the creative genius within us and upon all of the spiritual gifts available (see Moroni 10:8–19; D&C 46:8–30; 1 Corinthians 12:8–11).

We know that something must be created spiritually before it can be created temporarily (see Moses 3:5–7; that is, the goal is pictured within the mind's eye and the process of achieving the goal is previewed mentally. We do this by anticipating all of the hurdles that lie between us and our goal and by picturing ourselves jumping those hurdles. We then describe the "spiritual creation" in writing, step by step, until the full plan of action is created in fact.

To accomplish our Book of Mormon reading goal, we can take a sheet from the calendar and plot our plan of action. We calculate that the task will be completed in thirty days if we read eighteen pages a day.

We mark daily reading assignments on the sheet, such as Friday, January 1 – Title page through 1 Nephi 5. Once the reading plan is charted, we place it on a bulletin board or some other highly visible space. The visualization of the goal and plan will create enthusiasm for the task and serve as a constant reminder of the goal and daily expectancies. Perhaps a picture of a Book of Mormon event could even be posted for visualization purposes.

Step 4: Work diligently to reach the objective. We read day by day and reach our goal. We do not allow outside influences to disrupt our progress. In the process of reading and pursuing the goal, we monitor our progress daily. This monitoring is called verification. To verify is to establish the accuracy or reality of something. If the reading lags, we know to accelerate our efforts. If the reading exceeds expectations, through verification, we can adjust the goal to maintain its challenge.

Few things in life are more exhilarating or motivating than the attainment of a worthwhile goal. It stirs positive thinking ("I can succeed"), encourages the establishment of higher standards or expectations ("I can do more and better work"), and builds self-esteem ("I am a successful person").

These four things blended together (goals, positive thinking, high standards or expectations, self-esteem) constitute the keys to personal motivation.

Much more could be said about the process of goal setting, planning, and striving. Many books have been written on this subject. A number of companies have been organized to market tapes and self-study materials, all designed to help people become goal setters and successful planners. So it should be understood that what I have presented in this chapter about goals and plans is selective and sketchy at best.

I am sometimes offended by those who approach goal setting and goal striving as an exact science. Such people maintain that their processes will almost magically enable us to sell more books, pants, petroleum, and other things. They would also have us believe that these processes are the last word in teaching the gospel or winning souls.

We who are "soldiers of the spirit" understand perfectly the need for purpose and organization in our work. We also know that some ideas conceived by well-meaning people may have some virtue when related to our Church service, providing, of course, that such ideas are based upon correct principles. But, ours is a spiritual work governed by powers beyond paper, pants, and petroleum. We teach truth; we call people to repentance; we change lives; and we invite all to come unto Christ. Our challenge is to do all of this as effectively as possible without forcing minds, hoodwinking listeners, or offending agency. All that we do, including using goals, plans, and so on, must be done in accord with divine will, sacred purposes, and principles of righteousness.

Someone said, "Without some goal and some effort to reach it, no man can live." I subscribe to that thought if a few words are added. I would say it this way: "Without some worthy goal and some honest effort to reach it, no one can live fully."

Madison Square Garden

When I was a young man, I set a goal that helped direct my life. I want to share it with you because it reinforces all I have said about goals.

Soon after I turned fourteen years of age, I was ordained a teacher in the Aaronic Priesthood and was assigned as a ward teacher (now a home teacher). The Melchizedek Priesthood member appointed as my companion was Melvin Jensen, a man several years my senior.

Brother Jensen assumed the lead in scheduling the appointments and conducting the discussions in the homes. However, he did involve me in the visits in such a way as to provide me positive experiences.

One night as we walked toward the final appointment for the evening, Mel paused with me under a street light and engaged me in conversation. Among other things, he asked me questions about my future. One specific question was, "What is your great ambition in life?"

I hesitated momentarily—not because I didn't have a goal in mind, but because I feared that my response might sound silly to him. Mel spoke some words of reassurance and won my complete trust. So I said what was in my heart: "Someday, I hope to play basketball in Madison Square Garden."

There was an awkward silence. I don't believe Brother Jensen expected the kind of answer I gave. Thank goodness, however, he didn't laugh at my honest expression. If he had, I believe my hopes and dreams would have been dealt a crushing blow. Instead, Mel placed his big hand upon my shoulder and said: "That's wonderful, Carlos. I know you can do it." He added further encouragement by commenting on my size and ability; and he promised me that if I would keep myself clean and practice consistently, someday my dream would come true.

113

Brother Jensen's words of confidence lifted me more than I can describe. I had shared an intimate, heartfelt desire with someone I trusted and admired, and that person had, in turn, expressed faith in my ability to perform.

When our visits were completed that night, I said goodnight to my home teaching companion and ran home. Mother was in the kitchen as I entered the house, and I wasted little time in telling her about the conversation with Mel. She, too, was surprised to learn about my secret ambition.

Although my mother's interest in sports was less than avid over the years, she had learned to tolerate the "game talk" and the "Monday quarterback" commentaries of her husband and four active sons, and her interest in me was genuine. She said some reassuring things and wondered just how much I knew about Madison Square Garden. I confessed that I knew very little about the place. "If the Garden is related to your goal," she commented, "why don't you become better acquainted with it?" She suggested that I might want to collect newspaper and magazine clippings of pictures and articles involving Madison Square Garden. So, with her help and encouragement, in the succeeding months I filled my scrapbook and became somewhat of an authority on New York City's Madison Square Garden.

My dream caused me to train consistently. I tried hard to keep my body clean and to improve my abilities. I didn't want any bad habits or physical weaknesses to prevent me from reaching my goal. I recall shooting baskets by the hour, in all kinds of weather, at a hoop attached to an apple tree in my father's orchard. I was never alone, for the surrounding trees seemed like grandstands filled with cheering people as I lived my fantasy.

As the years passed and basketball seasons came and went, I continued to pursue my goal. Following high school came military and other experiences, and gradually my enthusiasm for the scrapbook ebbed.

My enthusiasm for the goal itself, however, remained riveted in my mind. Whenever I practiced or played, there was always that dream of performing before thousands in Madison Square Garden. I remained pointed toward the dream.

In 1946, at the age of twenty, I enrolled at the University of Utah. That fall, as a freshman, I tried out for and won a place on the varsity basketball team. At Christmastime, we toured in the eastern part of the United States. Part of our tour included a game in Madison Square Garden.

Entering the Garden that first time was almost like returning home, for in my mind and heart I had been there many times.

Later that same basketball season, in March 1947, I returned to Madison Square Garden with the University of Utah team to participate in the National Invitation Tournament (NIT). Thanks to a strong starting lineup consisting of Arnie Ferrin, Vern Gardner, Wat Misaka, Fred Weidner, and Leon Watson, we won the tournament.

Immediately following our victory — on the playing floor of Madison Square Garden — my teammates and I were presented with beautiful Bulova wristwatches.

I've worn my wristwatch for many years. Each time I look at it, I'm reminded of the pulling power of a well-defined goal. I'm reminded of the strength and resolution that come when a goal is verbalized and visualized. And I'm reminded of the important role that family and friends play in shaping lives.

I do pray that what I have written may help you in setting and accomplishing your goals. I do want you to be in charge of your life, and I do want you to succeed. You will, of course, want to pray about the thoughts I have shared and make proper applications of the principles pertaining to goal setting that seem right to you and those who preside over you.

Chapter Twelve

Seeking Earnestly
the Best Gifts

The Lord has not left us alone in our service to him. He has given us many resources to help us in our callings. One of the most important of these is the gifts of the Spirit, which will expand our powers to serve beyond our natural abilities. I assure you that such gifts of the Spirit are available to you, and to all who serve the Lord, if you seek them earnestly in accord with divine will.

Personal Reflections

As I think of spiritual gifts or gifts of the Spirit, my mind centers upon several people in the Church with whom I have shared special — even faith-promoting — experiences. I refer to people who have displayed unusual inner gifts, talents, and powers. I remember a missionary companion of many years ago who possessed the gift of tongues. He mastered three languages while the rest of us were struggling to grasp the rudiments of one. I also recall participating in the

117

miraculous healing of a child who was desperately ill. Even though the attending physician had declared that death was imminent, my missionary companion, through the power of the holy priesthood and the exercise of supreme faith, prolonged life.

I remember a student associate of mine at the university in my undergraduate years who served as a spiritual physician to my family. At the time, we had a son who was plagued with illness, and we were much too poor to pay for medicines and doctors. We called on this priesthood brother so many times to give blessings and to restore our son's health that we lovingly referred to him as "Bless-your-heart Barron."

I remember a missionary over whom I presided in Texas who possessed extraordinary gifts of faith and prophecy. Among other things, he was able to determine my transfers before I made them. You can imagine how popular he became with the other missionaries.

Most members of the Church, past and present, have seen evidences of spiritual gifts and divine powers. The annals of Church history contain many accounts of Saints in prior days receiving visions, miracles, and other heavenly manifestations; and, the personal journals and family histories of living Saints contain a generous sprinkling of accounts wherein spiritual powers have blessed the lives of members of the Church. One does wonder, however, if such evidences are received as frequently as they should be.

Signs of the True Church

Brigham Young said: "We are asked if signs follow the believer in our day as in days of old. We answer, they do. The blind see, the lame leap, the deaf hear, the gift of prophecy is manifest, also the gift of healing, the gift of revelation, the gift of tongues and the interpretation of tongues. Jesus said that these signs should follow them that believe. His Church and Kingdom always have these signs which follow the believer in all ages when the true Church is in existence" (*Journal of Discourses.* 26 vols. [London: Latter-day Saints' Book Depot, 1854–86], 12:208).

The presence of spiritual gifts, as mentioned by President Young, is evidence of the true Church and true priesthood power. On the other hand, the absence of spiritual gifts is indicative of apostasy, spiritual famine, and the withdrawal of God's power. Note the words of John Wesley, one of the Protestant reformers, who recognized the relationship between gifts of the Holy Ghost and the living church of Christ: "It does not appear that these extraordinary gifts of the Holy Ghost were common in the Church for more than two or three centuries. We seldom hear of them after that fatal period when the Emperor Constantine called himself a Christian. . . . From this time they almost totally ceased. . . . The Christians had no more of the Spirit of Christ than the other Heathens. . . . This was the real cause why the extraordinary gifts of the Holy Ghost were no longer to be found in the Christian Church; because the Christians were turned Heathens again, and had only a dead form left" ("The More Excellent Way," Sermon 89, in *The Works of John Wesley*, 14 vols., [1872; reprint ed., Grand Rapids, Michigan: Zondervan Publishing House, n.d.], 7:26–27).

The "dead form" mentioned by Wesley was verified by God himself when he described to Joseph Smith the religionists of the early nineteenth century: "They draw near to me with their lips, but their hearts are far from me, they teach for doctrines the commandments of men, having a form of godliness, *but they deny the power thereof*" (Joseph Smith–History 1:19; italics added).

I gather from the statements of Joseph Smith, Brigham Young, and John Wesley that gifts of the Holy Ghost are not only important but also essential. They are really (1) a mark of true believers, (2) a sign of the true church, and (3) manifestations of God's love. Knowing all of this, I understand more fully why the Apostle Paul wrote, "Now concerning spiritual gifts, brethren, I would not have you ignorant" (1 Corinthians 12:1). He might have said, "I would not have you without!"

It is my desire to share with you some thoughts that may help you overcome, at least in part, any ignorance or blind spots you may have about this subject of spiritual gifts. I also hope and pray that what I say will inspire you to seek more earnestly the best gifts that are available to all true believers. I would not have you ignorant of these blessings, nor would I have you go without them.

Sources of Information

Most of what I know about this holy subject and most of what I desire to share with you comes from three scriptural sources: the Doctrine and Covenants, section 46; the Book of Mormon, Moroni 10; and the New Testament, 1 Corinthians 12. All three of these companion accounts are much the same; nonetheless, each is distinct—each has its own setting, its own emphasis, and its own beauty.

In the Doctrine and Covenants, section 46, the instructions about gifts of the Spirit are preceded by instructions pertaining to Church worship services. Specifically, the Saints are told:

Conduct all meetings as directed and guided by the Holy Spirit.

Do not cast out those who are earnestly seeking after the kingdom.

Do not be seduced or deceived by evil spirits.

Preliminaries leading to the Book of Mormon, Moroni 10 material, consist of:

A description of how one obtains a testimony.

Reference to the power of the Holy Ghost.

The New Testament account, 1 Corinthians 12, also has a setting relating to worship services and the administration of the sacrament. It, too, makes reference to the Holy Spirit. Note Paul's lead statement: "I give you to understand, that no man speaking by the Spirit of God calleth Jesus accursed: and that no man can say that Jesus is the Lord, but by the Holy Ghost" (1 Corinthians 12:3).

So, it should be emphasized that when we speak of spiritual gifts, we are talking about the power of the Holy Ghost and the agency of the Spirit of Christ. Elder Bruce R. McConkie gives this explanation: "Moroni says that the gifts of God come from Christ, by the power of the Holy Ghost and by the Spirit of Christ. (Moro. 10). In other words, the gifts come by the power of that Spirit who is the Holy Ghost, but the Spirit of Christ (or light of Christ) is the agency through which the Holy Ghost operates" (*Mormon Doctrine*, p. 314).

President Romney adds: "The gifts of the spirit are given by the power of the Holy Ghost. Without the gift of the Holy Ghost, the manifestations of his gifts may not be enjoyed" (*Conference Report*, April 1956, p. 72).

Gifts of the Spirit

A master list of the gifts found in the three scriptural references mentioned above includes the following:

1. To know that Jesus Christ is the Son of God.

2. To believe on their words (the words of those who know that Jesus is the Christ).

3. Differences of administrations.

4. Diversities of operations.

5. The word of wisdom.

6. The word of knowledge.

7. Faith.
8. Gifts of healing.
9. Working of miracles.
10. Prophecy.
11. Discerning of spirits.
12. Speaking in tongues.
13. Interpretation of tongues.
14. Beholding of angels and ministering spirits.

This is not an exhaustive list of spiritual gifts. Many others can be found in the Standard Works. According to Elder McConkie, "In the fullest sense, they are infinite in number and endless in their manifestations" (*Mormon Doctrine,* p. 315).

I do, however, want to comment about one other gift that is treated in a special way. It is found in Mosiah 8:13–18:

> Now Ammon said unto him: I can assuredly tell thee, O king, of a man that can translate the records; for he has wherewith that he can look, and translate all records that are of ancient date; and it is a gift from God. And the things are called interpreters, and no man can look in them except he be commanded, lest he should look for that he ought not and he should perish. And whosoever is commanded to look in them, the same is called seer.
>
> And behold, the king of the people who are in the land of Zarahemla is the man that is commanded to do these things, and who has this high gift from God.
>
> And the king said that a seer is greater than a prophet.
>
> And Ammon said that a seer is a revelator and a prophet also; and a gift which is greater can no man have, except he should possess the power of God, which no man can; yet a man may have great power given him from God.
>
> But a seer can know of things which are past, and also of things which are to come, and by them shall all things be revealed, or, rather, shall secret things be made man-

ifest, and hidden things shall come to light, and things which are not known shall be made known by them, and also things shall be made known by them which otherwise could not be known.

Thus God has provided a means that man, through faith, might work mighty miracles; therefore he becometh a great benefit to his fellow beings.

One might ask: "Why are the lists basically the same?" Three possible explanations might be given:

1. Perhaps the Savior gave a sermon on gifts of the Spirit on both continents, to both the Jews and the Nephites.

2. Perhaps teachings on the gifts of the Spirit were recorded by a prophet in Old Testament times. Paul would have it through a lost manuscript, and Moroni would have it through the plates of Laban.

3. Perhaps both Paul and Moroni received revelations pertaining to spiritual gifts (see Daniel H. Ludlow, *A Companion to Your Study of the Book of Mormon* [Salt Lake City: Deseret Book Company, 1976], pp. 340–41).

The Commission to Seek Spiritual Gifts

I find it significant that God has given us more than a casual invitation to obtain spiritual gifts. There are seven very pointed and command-like statements that remind us of the absolute necessity to seek these gifts. In a sense, God has given us a commission to seek, a requirement to obtain, and a responsibility to share these spiritual gifts. Study the following declarations and notice the words italicized; each is strong and each denotes action on our part:

1. "*Seek* ye *earnestly* the best gifts" (D&C 46:8).

2. "*Lay hold* upon every good gift" (Moroni 10:30).

3. "*Covet earnestly* the best gifts" (1 Corinthians 12:31) (in this context, "covet earnestly" means "ardently desire").

4. "*Desire* spiritual gifts" (1 Corinthians 14:1).

5. *[Be] zealous* of spiritual gifts" (1 Corinthians 14:12) ("zealous" means enthusiastic in this case).

6. "This is thy gift; *apply unto it,* and blessed art thou" (D&C 8:4).

7. "*Ask of God,* who giveth liberally. . . . He that asketh in the Spirit, asketh according to the will of God" (D&C 46:7, 30).

The injunction is to "seek earnestly," "lay hold upon," "covet earnestly," "desire," "be zealous of," "apply unto it," and "ask of God." It isn't a proposition of, "If you have the time, do it," or, "If you have the inclination, try it." It isn't that at all. We are commanded to seek and cultivate gifts of the Spirit!

Why Are Spiritual Gifts Given?

One might ask: "Why are spiritual gifts given? What is their purpose or role in the divine scheme of things?" Once again, let us turn to the scriptures for an answer.

The Lord admonishes us, "[Always remember] for what they are given" (D&C 46:8). If we bear in mind the reasons why God endows us with such gifts, our motives for requesting them will more likely remain pure, and our tendencies to abuse those powers lessened.

Here are instructions from on high that help explain why spiritual gifts are given (certain words are italicized for emphasis):

1. "*For the benefit of those who love me* and keep *all* my commandments, and him that seeketh so to do" (D&C 46:9).

2. "*That all may be benefited that seek* or that ask of me" (D&C 46:9).

3. "They are given by the manifestations of the Spirit of God unto men, *to profit them*" (Moroni 10:8).

4. "And all these gifts come from God, *for the benefit of the children of God*" (D&C 46:26).

5. "Seek that *ye may excel to the edifying of the church*" (1 Corinthians 14:12).

6. "For I long to see you, that I may impart unto you some spiritual gift, to the end *ye may be established*" (Romans 1:11).

7. "That *every member may be profited* thereby" (D&C 46:29).

Spiritual gifts properly sought, properly received, and properly shared will establish faith, profit those who love God, and edify the Church. Elder Bruce R. McConkie provides this statement of purpose: "Their purpose is to enlighten, encourage, and edify the faithful so that they will inherit peace in this life and be guided toward eternal life in the world to come. Their presence is proof of the divinity of the Lord's work; where they are not found, there the Church and kingdom of God is not" (*Mormon Doctrine,* p. 314).

I would stress that God's gifts are not dispersed or cast about freely into the wind. They are reserved for those who love him and keep his commandments. They are given to benefit the children of God—not the children of men. To place spiritual gifts before nonbelievers would be like casting pearls before swine. That which is holy should be reserved for those who recognize its worth and who will give it reverence (see Matthew 7:6).

How Many Gifts?

Some people wonder where they were when the spiritual gifts were distributed. Perhaps some even feel that they were completely overlooked. At times I have envied the gifts made apparent in the lives of those around me; and, on occasion, I have wondered why I haven't received more of an endowment. However, as I have studied this subject and my knowledge of gifts has increased, I have been led to repent of these past feelings, for I now know that:

1. "All have not every gift given unto them; for there are many gifts, and to every man is given a gift by the Spirit of God. To some is given one, and to some is given another" (D&C 46:11–12).

2. "Every man hath his proper [own] gift of God, one after this manner, and another after that" (1 Corinthians 7:7).

3. "Unto *some* it may be given to have all those gifts, *that there may be a head,* in order that every member may be profited thereby" (D&C 46:29; italics added).

I also now know that, through the Spirit, God divides "to every man severally, according as he will" (Moroni 10:17).

Is it possible that certain gifts lie dormant within you? Perhaps you haven't mined deeply enough within your own soul to discover the golden gifts that reside there. Maybe you haven't heeded sufficiently the subtle intimations of the Spirit that provide clues to the inner powers. How appropriate was Paul's warning to Timothy: "Neglect not the gift that is in thee." (1 Timothy 4:14).

Paul stimulated the thinking of the Saints in Corinth by asking: "Have all the gifts of healing? do all speak with tongues? do all interpret?" (1 Corinthians 12:30). In the process, he likened members of the Church to members of the human body. He suggested that all members are essential and all have their place. Likewise, he implied that each member of the Church has a gift and some worthy function to perform. His appeal to all, however, was, "But covet earnestly the best gifts: and yet shew I unto you a more excellent way" (1 Corinthians 12:31).

I am told that after learning one language, it is easy to

learn another, for often the structure and form of one is similar to the structure and form of another. Would this not also hold true for spiritual gifts? If we perfect our faith, will this not also help us in healings? Will not a gift of tongues provide insights to the interpretation of languages? All gifts are from God and come by the Holy Ghost, so it seems reasonable that the more consistently we court that holy influence, the more likely it is that our spiritual gifts will be multiplied and strengthened.

How to Acquire Spiritual Gifts

How can we acquire spiritual gifts? Again, we should refer to the three basic scriptures. Each outlines a process not unrelated to the other. Altogether the three processes give us clear and specific direction.

All missionaries are acquainted with the four steps to a testimony as recorded in the Book of Mormon. The truth seeker is asked to—

1. *Read* the word of God.
2. *Remember* God's goodness to his children.
3. *Ponder* the things read and remembered.
4. *Ask God* if these things are not true.

The promise given is that, at the conclusion of these actions, "by the power of the Holy Ghost," the person may "know the truth of all things" (Moroni 10:3–5).

Picking up with "Ask God," let us turn now to the Doctrine and Covenants. This record states these steps in asking for spiritual gifts:

1. Ask in Spirit.
2. Ask with a sincere heart and real intent.
3. Ask according to the will of God.
4. Ask in the name of Christ.
5. Give thanks to God.

Practice virtue and holiness before God continually (D&C 46:28–33; see also Moroni 10:4).

After we have read, remembered, pondered, and prayed (asked), we must follow the remaining directions found in the New Testament:

1. Meditate upon the gifts promised.
2. Give ourselves wholly to them.
3. Take heed unto ourselves and doctrine.
4. Save ourselves and those that hear us (see 1 Timothy 4:15–16).

As stated previously, these actions attract the Holy Spirit. And, it is through that Spirit that gifts and powers are extended.

If we hope to acquire good gifts, we must strengthen the Spirit. This is done best by—

1. *Reading and pondering the scriptures.* Scripture reading does for the Spirit what calisthenics do for the physical body.

2. *Fasting and praying.* These are aerobic-type exercises for the Spirit. They pump life-giving powers throughout the system and must be done frequently.

3. *Living virtuously and having faith.* Light cleaves to light, and virtue attracts the Holy Spirit. Faith claims the unseen influences.

It should be remembered that the disciples of Christ failed on one occasion to heal a man vexed with an evil spirit. The Savior taught them: "If ye have faith as a grain of mustard seed, ye shall say unto this mountain, Remove hence to yonder place; and it shall remove; and nothing shall be impossible unto you. Howbeit this kind goeth not out but by prayer and fasting" (Matthew 17:20–21).

Warnings

I would be derelict in my presentation if I didn't share some words of warning related to the Spirit and spiritual gifts. Again, I shall lean upon the scriptures. To begin with, the Lord said:

"I would exhort you that ye deny not the power of God; for he worketh by power, according to the faith of the children of men, the same today and tomorrow, and forever" (Moroni 10:7).

"I exhort you, my brethren, that ye deny not the gifts of God" (Moroni 10:8).

Next, he warns against unbelief:

"All these gifts . . . never will be done away, even as long as the world shall stand, only according to the unbelief of the children of men" (Moroni 10:19).

"If the day cometh that the power and gifts of God shall be done away among you, it shall be because of unbelief" (Moroni 10:24).

Thirdly, he has a word for the sign seekers:

"[Gifts are given] not for a sign that they may consume it upon their lusts" (D&C 46:9).

Some commentators have added: "There is one kind of prayer that God does not grant—prayer for gifts to gratify carnal desires" (*Doctrine and Covenants Commentary*, rev. ed. [Cambridge, Mass.: Cambridge University Press, 1951], p. 272).

Fourth, he implies that gifts may also come from evil or Satanic sources, for he warns, "Touch not the evil gift, nor the unclean thing" (Moroni 10:30).

And, finally, he instructs: "Remember that without faith you can do nothing; therefore ask in faith. Trifle [joke or play] not with these things; do not ask for that which you ought not" (D&C 8:10).

You will recall that Nephi of old labored with such "unwearyingness" that God promised, "I will bless thee forever; and I will make thee mighty in word and in deed, in faith and in works; yea, even that all things shall be done unto thee according to thy word, *for thou shalt not ask that which is contrary to my will*" (Helaman 10:5; italics added).

Conclusion

The gifts of the Spirit have been referred to as tools of the priesthood, and rightly so. They are to the priesthood holder what a hammer is to a carpenter, a scalpel is to a physician, and a plow is to a farmer. But they are available not only to bearers of the priesthood, but to all who seek them in righteousness. All who deal with spiritual matters must be equipped with spiritual gifts and Godly powers.

How can a Sunday School teacher perform effectively in the Church unless he or she knows that Jesus Christ is the Son of God? How can a quorum leader function properly without administrative helps? How can a missionary bear witness without the spirit of prophecy and without the gift of tongues? How can a bishop preside over a ward and tend the needs of his flock without the ability to discern spirits? How can parents rear children in righteousness without the word of knowledge? And, how can any of us cope successfully with life and its challenges without the gifts of faith and ministering spirits?

When we ignore the spiritual dimension of our souls, we bind ourselves with the weaknesses of the flesh. But when we recognize the divine spark that resides within us and allow that spark to be kindled by heavenly fires, almost limitless powers are unleashed. Moses did not become the great deliverer until spiritual powers were ignited within him; Joseph Smith, the farm boy, became the Prophet of the Restoration because he sought light and truth; and, we will never rise to the heights that Saints of the living God should attain until we seek and obtain spiritual gifts.

A number of years ago, Elder George Q. Cannon inquired of the Saints: "How many of you, my brethren and sisters, are seeking for these gifts that God has promised to bestow? How many of you, when you bow before your Heavenly Father in your family circle or in your secret places, contend for these gifts to be bestowed upon you? . . . There is not that seeking for the gift of healing and for the gift to be healed that there ought to be among the Saints. And so with other gifts and graces that God has placed in His Church for His people. . . . Let us seek for these gifts. . . . Let us seek for them with all our might, mind, and strength" (*Millennial Star,* April 23, 1894, pp. 260–61).

I pray that we will appreciate more fully the actuality of spiritual gifts. May we seek earnestly the best gifts and use them in fighting against spiritual wickedness and powers of darkness. Well might we remember that God is our Father and that he stands ready to endow us with his gifts, for it is promised:

> Ask, and it shall be given you; seek, and ye shall find; knock, and it shall be opened unto you:
>
> For every one that asketh receiveth; and he that seeketh findeth; and to him that knocketh it shall be opened.
>
> Or what man is there of you, whom if his son ask bread, will he give him a stone?
>
> Or if he ask a fish, will he give him a serpent?
>
> If ye then, being evil, know how to give good gifts unto your children, how much more shall your Father which is in heaven give good things to them that ask him? (Matthew 7:9–11.)

I bear witness of spiritual gifts and urge you to seek them earnestly.

Chapter Thirteen

Teaching by the Spirit

One of the most common and yet one of the most important callings in the Church is that of teaching, which has been aptly referred to as the Master's art. Such reference is justified in many ways. Our Lord and Savior, Jesus the Christ, was the greatest teacher of all time. He lived and taught in a most persuasive manner, using parables, stories, scriptures, vivid language, and all the other tools needed to convey truth and win followers. He read the thoughts of others, asked and answered searching questions, healed broken hearts, condemned hypocrites, and lifted others with both words and hands. I echo the words of Nicodemus: "We know that [Christ was a master] teacher come from God: for no man [could] do these miracles . . . except God be with him" (John 3:2).

The act of teaching is more than a skill that can be mastered through practice and endless repetition. It is an art that requires a careful blend of sensitivity, thought, understanding, love, and goodness by one whose "brush and strokes" are guided by heavenly powers.

Christ is the exemplar for all Saints, especially for those who have been called to "declare his generation," "publish peace," and declare "good tidings of good" (Mosiah 15:10, 14). Such teachers must seek to follow him and to be even as he is (see 3 Nephi 27:27). Moreover, they must "observe to do, even as [Christ has] done" (3 Nephi 18:6). This means that those who are called to teach must do so with power and authority, after the manner of the Savior (see Matthew 7:29), so that listeners will say, "Did not our heart burn within us, while he talked with us by the way, and while he opened to us the scriptures?" (Luke 24:32.)

Teaching—a Transfusion

Ralph Waldo Emerson wrote: "The same reality pervades all teaching. The man may teach by doing, and not otherwise. If he can communicate himself, he can teach, but not by words. He teaches who gives, and he learns who receives. There is no teaching until the pupil is brought into the same state or principal in which you are; *a transfusion takes place;* he is you, and you are he; then is a teaching" (In *The Works of R. W. Emerson,* [Roslyn, N.Y, Black's Readers Service Co.], p. 135; italics added).

A number of gems can be mined from this quotation. As it implies, actions do speak louder than words; we cannot give away that which we do not already possess; and, teachers must seek an understanding of their pupil's innermost needs and desires. Yet, the "crown jewel" found in the words of Emerson relates to the transfusion that must take place in the teaching process. Such occurs when eye meets eye, hearts beat in unison, and one spirit speaks to another in the quiet language of the soul.

The Spirit of Truth

The spirit-to-spirit dialogue and the transfusion of testimony alluded to above are described by the Lord in a modern revelation. He declared to the Prophet Joseph Smith and the elders of the Church:

> Unto what were ye ordained?
> To preach my gospel by the Spirit, even the Comforter which was sent forth to teach the truth. . . .
> Verily I say unto you, he that is ordained of me and sent forth to preach the word of truth by the Comforter, in the Spirit of truth, doth he preach it by the Spirit of truth or some other way?
> And if it be by some other way it is not of God.
> And again, he that receiveth the word of truth, doth he receive it by the Spirit of truth or some other way?
> If it be some other way it is not of God. . . .
> Wherefore, he that preacheth and he that receiveth, understand one another, and both are edified and rejoice together. (D&C 50:13–14, 17–20, 22.)

Of course, some instruction may occur with or without the aid of the Spirit. The spread of information mouth to ear in a spiritless style or the disclosure of data in a matter-of-fact manner happens all the time and has mixed impact upon us. On the other hand, edification occurs only under the influence of the Spirit. It takes place through mouth-to-heart communication and via the Spirit of truth. The participating parties are inspired and built up morally, giving rise to long-lasting resolves and results. One who is edified by instruction responds as King Benjamin's congregation responded: "Yea, we believe all the words which thou hast spoken unto us; and also, we know of their surety and truth, because of the Spirit of the Lord Omnipotent, which has wrought a mighty change in us, or in our hearts, that we

134

have no more disposition to do evil, but to do good continually" (Mosiah 5:2).

King Benjamin was a masterful teacher as evidenced by his ability to instruct and edify simultaneously.

Preparing to Teach

So, in light of all that has been said about teaching, transfusion, and truth, what must you do to prepare yourself to teach by the Spirit with power and authority? Four scriptures come to mind that you should ponder:

1. *Seek:* "Seek not to declare my word, but first seek to obtain my word, and then shall your tongue be loosed; then, if you desire, you shall have my Spirit and my word, yea, the power of God unto the convincing of men" (D&C 11:21).

There is an inseparable connection between the word of God and the power of God (see Alma 31:5). And, there is a kinship between desire, honest desire, and the acquisition of the Spirit. When all of these elements are combined, according to the Lord's prescription, tongues are loosened and people are led "to do that which [is] just" (Alma 31:5; see also Alma 26:22).

One who attempts to teach before obtaining truth is as powerless as the one who draws string upon a target without an arrow in place.

2. *Pray:* "And the Spirit shall be given unto you by the prayer of faith; and if ye receive not the Spirit ye shall not teach" (D&C 42:14).

These words should not be construed by missionaries as an excuse not to teach. They should be interpreted as a command to pray and to obtain the Spirit. If one prayer of faith is not sufficient, then perhaps two or more will bring the desired results.

3. *Speak:* "After ye had received the Holy Ghost ye could

speak with the tongue of angels. . . . Angels speak by the power of the Holy Ghost; wherefore, they speak the words of Christ. Wherefore, I said unto you, feast upon the words of Christ; for behold, the words of Christ will tell you all things what ye should do" (2 Nephi 32:2–3).

It is nice to speak another tongue or a second language. But, no tongue or language is more essential to the success of a missionary than the one associated with angels. Those who acquire this tongue become mighty proselyters like Wilford Woodruff, the Apostle Paul, and others.

4. *Teach:* "Teach ye diligently and my grace shall attend you, that you may be instructed more perfectly . . . that ye may . . . magnify the calling whereunto I have called you, and the mission with which I have commissioned you" (D&C 88:78–80).

Those who are diligent are constant and persistent; those who do their full share merit the goodness and grace of God; and those who magnify their callings are forever expending their knowledge, honing their skills, and strengthening their abilities. All of these behaviors build the servants of Christ and enable them to "speak because of the spirit which is in [them]" (see 2 Nephi 25:11).

A Teaching Sequence

Among the many challenges faced by teachers are these: (1) helping people recognize the changes in their lives as they more fully live the gospel, and (2) helping them recognize and respond to the Spirit that is working upon them. Since these two challenges have bearing upon teaching responsibilities, I desire to share a personal experience that may cast light upon the subject at hand.

A few years ago, a missionary companionship referred to me a young couple with two children who were investigating the Church. This family had been taught a number of lessons and had attended Church on several occasions; but, they would not accept the invitation to be baptized and to join the Church.

Prayer

After a brief exchange of niceties and a prayer, I was impressed to ask the husband, "How did you feel about prayer before you met the missionaries?"

"Not much," he replied. "Until recently I seldom prayed."

I inquired, "Do you pray now? Is prayer an essential aspect of your daily living?"

"Oh, yes," he said. "We pray all the time. We bless the food before each meal; we have family prayer each day; and I pray frequently about my work."

I commended the couple for cultivating this sanctifying habit, and I invited the husband to read aloud the words of the Lord contained in 2 Nephi 32:8–9. He read:

> And now, my beloved brethren, I perceive that ye ponder still in your hearts; and it grieveth me that I must speak concerning this thing. For if ye would hearken unto the Spirit which teacheth a man to pray ye would know that ye must pray; for the evil spirit teacheth not a man to pray, but teacheth him that he must not pray.
>
> But behold, I say unto you that ye must pray always, and not faint; that ye must not perform any thing unto the Lord save in the first place ye shall pray unto the Father in the name of Christ, that he will consecrate thy performance unto thee, that thy performance may be for the welfare of thy soul (2 Nephi 32:8–9).

I then asked the man, "According to the word of God, what spirit teaches a man not to pray?"

"The evil spirit," he answered.

"So what spirit have you been listening to?" I pressed.

He answered, "I have been influenced by the good spirit or the Spirit of God."

I thanked the investigator for his simple expression of testimony about the concept of prayer.

Enlightenment

My next questions were also addressed to the man. I said, "How deep was your knowledge of God and his plan of salvation before the missionaries made contact with you?"

He shrugged and admitted, "Our knowledge of God and his purposes were very limited indeed. We knew little about premortal, mortal, or postmortal life."

I asked, "Has your understanding of spiritual things increased in recent weeks?"

"Oh, yes," was the response. "The missionaries have taught us many wonderful truths."

"Let's read again from holy writ a scripture that has bearing upon what you have just said," I added. "Turn to Alma 32:28, 34." This is what he read:

> Now, we will compare the word unto a seed. Now, if ye give place, that a seed may be planted in your heart, behold, if it be a true seed, or a good seed, if ye do not cast it out by your unbelief, that ye will resist the Spirit of the Lord, behold, it will begin to swell within your breasts; and when you feel these swelling motions, ye will begin to say within yourselves — It must needs be that this is a good seed, or that the word is good, for it beginneth to enlarge my soul; yea, it beginneth to enlighten my understanding, yea, it beginneth to be delicious to me. . . .
>
> And now, behold, is your knowledge perfect? Yea, your knowledge is perfect in that thing, and your faith is dormant; and this because you know, for ye know that the word hath swelled your souls, and ye also know that it hath sprouted up, that your understanding doth begin to

be enlightened, and your mind doth begin to expand (Alma 32:28, 34).

I said, "This reference from the Book of Mormon reminds us that, if the seed or word is good, it will enlarge our souls and enlighten our understandings, providing we do not resist the Spirit of the Lord."

It required little persuasion for the investigator to acknowledge that the "word" or seed shared with him by the missionaries was true and good, and that he had felt the Spirit during the teaching process.

Goodness

The third series of questions was directed to the woman of the house. I began, "Your husband is undoubtedly a good man or you would not have married him. But, how has his role as a husband and father changed since the missionaries came into your life?"

She did not hesitate to say, "He has definitely been more loving and considerate to me and the children as we have studied the restored gospel."

"Thank you for your honesty," I remarked. "Please turn once more to the book we refer to as 'Another Testament of Christ,' the Book of Mormon, and read from Ether 4:11–12." She read:

> But he that believeth these things which I have spoken, him will I visit with the manifestations of my Spirit, and he shall know and bear record. For because of my Spirit he shall know that these things are true; for it persuadeth men to do good.
> And whatsoever thing persuadeth men to do good is of me; for good cometh of none save it be of me. I am the same that leadeth men to all good; he that will not believe my words will not believe me—that I am; and he that will not believe me will not believe the Father who sent

me. For behold, I am the Father, I am the light, and the life, and the truth of the world (Ether 4:11–12).

I inquired, "According to the scripture you have just read, what Spirit persuades a person to do good?"

"The Spirit of God," she replied.

"Then," I continued, "what Spirit has been working upon your husband?"

She willingly testified that a new and building spirit had entered their home and that this same spirit had changed her life and her husband's life rather dramatically.

Christ

Finally, I spoke again to the man and asked him about his faith in Christ. He confessed that before his meetings with the missionaries, his faith had wavered and that he had entertained serious doubts concerning the Savior. He stated, however, that the teachings and testimonies of the missionaries had strengthened considerably his faith.

I requested that he read for us the following inspired words from modern scriptures:

> Take heed, my beloved brethren, that ye do not judge that which is evil to be of God, or that which is good and of God to be of the devil.
>
> For behold, my brethren, it is given unto you to judge, that ye may know good from evil; and the way to judge is as plain, that ye may know with a perfect knowledge, as the daylight is from the dark night.
>
> For behold, the Spirit of Christ is given to every man, that he may know good from evil; wherefore, I show unto you the way to judge; for every thing which inviteth to do good, and to persuade to believe in Christ, is sent forth by the power and gift of Christ; wherefore ye may know with a perfect knowledge it is of God. (Moroni 7:14–16.)

At the close of his reading, I asked, "What Spirit invites us to do good and persuades us to believe in Christ?"

"It is obvious," he answered. "It is the Spirit of Christ given to all men—just as the scripture indicated."

I expressed thanks for what he said and added, "What spirit has been influencing and teaching and edifying your lives these past few weeks?"

Rather solemnly and humbly he responded, "The Spirit of God."

To clinch the conversation, I said to the investigators, "You have testified to me four times about prayer, enlightenment, goodness, and Christ. You have acknowledged that a new and precious spirit has entered your lives. You have rediscovered faith—living faith—and have obtained a new perspective and a fresh purpose for living. You will, therefore, be baptized and do whatever is requisite in joining the Church, won't you?"

The family accepted the invitation and joined with the Saints.

Implications of the Teaching Sequence

A number of lessons can be learned from the above exchange with investigators and the four "Indicators of Truth" mentioned. Here are but a few:

1. Those who teach by the Spirit must center their instruction upon the gospel truths lodged in the holy scriptures, especially the Book of Mormon. It is this book that verifies the restoration of the gospel through the Prophet Joseph Smith. It is this book that entices the Spirit and draws people closer to God. And, it is this book that helps us to avoid fruitless arguments about points of doctrine.

2. Those who teach by the Spirit must help people recognize the subtle changes that occur in their lives as they grow in the truth. Sometimes these changes come so quietly

and so slowly that they are overlooked, unless someone takes the time to point them out.

3. Those who teach by the Spirit must provide people an opportunity to express themselves and to vocalize newfound truths. People may hear a precept or receive exposure to a concept, but they do not internalize the teachings until they vocalize and live them.

4. Those who teach by the Spirit must guide people in the expression of testimonies, however simple and brief such expressions may seem at first. Testimonies as succinct as, "I now know the virtue of prayer," "My knowledge of God has increased," "I'm a better person than I was a few months ago," or, "I have gained a love for Christ" become the roots of more abiding testimonies that grow in time through obedience and service. This is true not only in one-on-one teaching, such as missionary discussions or priesthood interviews, but also in the classroom.

5. Those who teach by the Spirit must seek commitments from their students and help them live on a higher level. Each commitment or resolve kept is a step upward in the direction of becoming a Saint. People must become doers of the word as well as hearers if gospel teachings are to bear fruit.

Conclusion

I once knew a missionary who suffered red-faced confusion in his initial teaching experience as a full-time missionary. He was unable to locate a reference in Jeremiah when called upon by his senior companion. He was unable to converse intelligently with the investigators or bear personal testimony. Afterward, he admitted that his failure and embarrassment were related to his lack of humility, ignorance of the scriptures, poor teaching skills, and a "spotty" relationship with the Holy Spirit.

He was, however, driven to his knees and prompted to beg God's forgiveness for being such an unprepared representative. That same day, he pledged to the Lord that he would become a student of the scriptures, strive to master teaching skills, and seek to establish a companionship with the Spirit. In time, the miracle happened. He became one of the most effective missionaries I have ever met, for he learned how to teach by the Spirit and apply the Master's art. He was able to transfuse light and truth into the lives of others, for he spoke by the Spirit of truth, used the tongue of angels, and served diligently.

God bless you. May you do likewise and find added joy and success in your labors.

Chapter Fourteen

Coming unto Christ: The Book of Mormon Approach

The Lord's message to all people everywhere is "Come unto me" (Matthew 11:28). This is also the invitation you have been commissioned to extend in behalf of God and his holy cause—to "come unto Christ, and be perfected in him" (Moroni 10:32).

The Christus

At the entrance of the harbor at Lisbon, Portugal, is an immense statue of Christ. It stands high upon a hill and can be seen from afar. The Savior is depicted with arms outstretched, as if he were hanging upon a cross. His posture is rigid, and his appearance is ominous.

In a chapel in Copenhagen, Denmark, is another statue of Jesus. It is referred to as the Christus. The Savior is shown looking compassionately downward with arms open and extended in a most inviting manner. This inspired depiction by Bertel Thorvaldsen seems to square with several scripture references, including, " . . . that this people had not repented that they might have been clasped in the arms of Jesus" (Mormon 5:11).

Whenever I think of the Savior, I picture him in my mind's eye with a soft smile upon his face and with his "arms of mercy . . . extended towards" all people. And, I can hear him say, "Come unto me and ye shall partake of the fruit of the tree of life; yea, ye shall eat and drink of the bread and the waters of life freely" (Alma 5:33–34).

Throughout the years, Christ's invitation—the divine invitation—has been spoken in various ways. To some he said, "Follow me" (Matthew 4:19); to others he said, "Come and see" (John 1:39); but always and to all people he has entreated, "Come unto [me] and partake of [my] goodness"; and "he denieth none that come unto him, black and white, bond and free, male and female; . . . all are alike unto God." (2 Nephi 26:33).

Jesus is the Christ. Of that fact I do attest. He is our Lord and Savior; he is "the author and the finisher of [our] faith" (Moroni 6:4). He is "the resurrection, and the life" (John 11:25). And, his name is the only name given "whereby salvation can come unto the children of men" (Mosiah 3:17). Hence, that beautiful and divine entreaty: "Come unto me and be ye saved" (3 Nephi 12:20).

The Real Issue

The real issue, therefore, is not whether we should come unto Christ. That is a given and established need. But, rather, the burning issue is: How do we come unto him?

The answer to this question is found in the Book of Mormon, another testament of Christ. Speaking of the latter days and the knowledge that would be given to the Gentiles, Nephi recorded, "They shall come to the knowledge of their Redeemer and the very points of his doctrine, that they may know how to come unto him and be saved" (1 Nephi 15:14). Nephi was referring to the instructions in the Book of Mormon that mark clearly the path leading to Christ.

How to Come unto Christ

These "how to" instructions that will move us closer to the Master and the eternal joy he promises include:

1. Coming "to the knowledge of [the] Redeemer and the very points of his doctrine" (1 Nephi 15:14).

2. Seeking "this Jesus of whom the prophets and apostles have written" (Ether 12:41).

3. Repenting and denying ourselves "of all ungodliness" (Moroni 10:32; 2 Nephi 2:10).

4. Entering the strait and narrow path through the gate of repentance and baptism (2 Nephi 31:17).

5. Loving "God with all [our] might, mind and strength" (Moroni 10:32).

6. Keeping "the commandments of the Father" (2 Nephi 31:10).

7. Following Christ and doing "the things which [we] have seen [him] do" (2 Nephi 31:12, Alma 5:35).

8. Offering our "whole souls as an offering unto him" (Omni 1:26).

9. Continuing "in fasting and prayer" (Omni 1:26).

10. Warning, expounding, exhorting, teaching, and inviting "all to come unto Christ" (D&C 20:59).

11. Coming to Christ "with full purpose of heart" (Jacob 6:5).

12. Pressing forward and enduring to the end (see 2 Nephi 31:20).

Yes, each time we read the scriptures, repent, obey a commandment, honor a covenant, utter a prayer, do an act of kindness, or bear testimony—each time we exercise our faith in any work of righteousness, we draw one step closer to Christ.

Five Approaches

Much more could be written about the twelve items listed above. Each is worthy of a chapter in and of itself. However, I want to emphasize five actions I feel are most pertinent to a calling in the Church:

1. *We must come unto Christ by reading the holy scriptures.* In the New Testament we read: "This is life eternal, that they might know thee the only true God, and Jesus Christ, whom thou hast sent" (John 17:3).

Another testament includes this pronouncement of intent: To "persuade men to come unto . . . God . . . and be saved" (1 Nephi 6:4).

The Prophet Joseph Smith promised that we would get nearer to the Lord by reading the Book of Mormon and by abiding by its precepts than by any other book (see the introduction to the Book of Mormon). Little wonder that the Lord exhorted all people to come unto God and to believe in prophesying and in revelations (see Omni 1:25).

When we search the scriptures, we not only learn of Christ and the plan of salvation, but we also can testify that we have heard his voice and know his words (see D&C 18:34–36).

Alma reminds us that a means has been provided for us to come unto Christ, even the word of Christ or recorded scripture. He said: "Behold, it is as easy to give heed to the word of Christ, which will point to you a straight course to eternal bliss, as it was for our fathers to give heed to this compass, which would point unto them a straight course to the promised land" (Alma 37:44).

2. *We must come unto Christ through repentance.* The Lord has said, "Repent, and I will receive you" and "repent

and come unto me" (Alma 5:33; 2 Nephi 28:32). "No unclean thing," we are told, "can dwell with God" (1 Nephi 10:21). Moreover, we are reminded that we would feel miserable to dwell with God under a consciousness of our own sins or filthiness (see Mormon 9:4–5).

Therefore, if we have hopes of standing in his holy presence, we must involve ourselves in continuous repentance. By doing so, each purging action or perfecting effort is a step in his direction. Each signifies acceptance of his invitation, "Come unto [me], and be perfected in [me], and deny yourselves of all ungodliness" (Moroni 10:32).

3. *We must come unto Christ through fasting and prayer.* One Book of Mormon writer echoed the divine invitation by saying, "Come unto him, and offer your whole souls as an offering unto him, and continue in fasting and prayer" (Omni 1:26).

Prayer is conversation with Deity. And, when it is coupled with the humbling process of fasting, our thoughts and spirits ascend ever Godward.

Thoughts generally precede the act, and our thoughts should more often be allowed to precede the word. So, controlling the inner impulses is one of our great challenges. This control can best be developed through quiet meditation and prayer.

I love the words of the hymn "Prayer is the Soul's Sincere Desire":

> *Prayer is the simplest form of speech . . .*
> *Prayer is the Christian's vital breath . . .*
> *Prayer, the sublimest strains that reach*
> *The Majesty on high.*
> (*Hymns*, no. 145.)

4. *We must come unto Christ through saving covenants and ordinances.* Jacob, who had obtained a personal witness

of Christ, declared, "Come with full purpose of heart" (Jacob 6:5).

Such fulness of purpose is signified through covenants and ordinances. We initiate our commitment to God by repenting and receiving the ordinance of baptism. We progress in our climb upward by receiving the Holy Ghost, participating in sacrament services, and receiving other ordinances. Ultimately, we go to the house of the Lord and participate in exalting ordinances and covenants that bridge heaven and earth and prepare us to enter into God's presence.

5. *We must come unto Christ through service to our fellowmen.* Note these instructions:

"I then, your Lord and Master, have washed your feet; ye also ought to wash one another's feet" (John 13:14).

"Whosoever will be great among you, let him be your minister; and whosoever will be chief among you, let him be your servant" (Matthew 20:26–27).

A modern revelation contains this important pronouncement: "They [Church members] are . . . to warn, expound, exhort, and teach, and invite all to come unto Christ" (D&C 20:59).

King Benjamin taught, "Behold, I tell you these things that ye may learn wisdom; that ye may learn that when ye are in the service of your fellow beings ye are only in the service of your God" (Mosiah 2:17).

God works through us to accomplish his purposes. We serve as proxies for him in performing his work and in blessing the lives of his children. In this process we become like him and approach the fulness of his stature.

Conclusion

There are those who wonder whether a person can have too much religion or become too righteous. I ask of such people, Can we draw too close to Christ?

There are those who say that the divine invitation applied only to people in the meridian of time. But I ask, "Is not a soul at this time as precious to God as a soul was two thousand years ago?" (see Alma 39:17–19).

Some years ago, a man asked one of our priesthood leaders, "What is your principal work or occupation?" Almost instinctively and without a moment's hesitation, the priesthood leader responded, "Preaching of Christ and him crucified."

"Can you live on that?" the inquirer pressed with a shocked look.

"I can't live without it," was the thrilling reply from one who loves the Lord more than life itself and is immersed in coming to Christ and inviting others to do so.

Some months ago, I was privileged to visit Gethsemane near Jerusalem. It was a lovely day—one that contributed to reflective thought and remembrance of Christ's suffering in our behalf. Among the other things I saw on that occasion was a plaque with this inscription:

> *Here now the Savior calleth thee in love,*
> *God calleth, calleth, calleth;*
> *Repent and come back home.*

The Savior continues to call people through you, in your calling. You have been commissioned to call people to him.

Some accept the divine invitation and attempt to come unto Christ. Others refuse his entreaty and turn away. But, the day will come when all will stand before Christ, whether they are ready or not, and be judged.

May we prepare for that day of accounting by coming closer to Christ each day we live. May we study the Book of Mormon and follow the plan of salvation outlined by God so that we can say at the appropriate time: "I soon go to the place of my rest, which is with my Redeemer; for I know that in him I shall rest. And I rejoice in the day when my mortal shall put on immortality, and shall stand before him; then shall I see his face with pleasure, and he will say unto me: Come unto me, ye blessed, there is a place prepared for you in the mansions of my Father. Amen" (Enos 1:27).

More than anything else, I want someday to return home and see his face with pleasure. I know that day will come if my approach to him is steady and consistent with his divine invitation.

I pray that you will come unto Christ each day that you live and serve, and that you will invite others to do the same.

Chapter Fifteen

Understanding and Overcoming Opposition

Those engaged in the work of the Lord will at some point encounter opposition from Satan and those who follow him. The war for the souls of God's children is real. As the Apostle Paul wrote, "We wrestle not against flesh and blood, but against principalities, against powers, against the rulers of the darkness of this world, against spiritual wickedness in high places" (Ephesians 6:12).

You must, therefore, be a "good soldier of Jesus Christ" and be prepared to endure "hardness," or opposition (2 Timothy 2:3). Please understand that few, if any, of those called to Church service have escaped exposure to the worldly opposition to the work of the Lord. Sometimes the opposition is light and easily brushed aside like a bothersome fly. At other times, however, the opposition is strong, planned, and very devious. And, if you are not properly prepared to make your stand against distracting influences, the devil and his henchmen can discourage you and limit your effectiveness (see Ephesians 6:11).

A Chinese Fable

On November 1, 1857, Elder George A. Smith delivered a memorable discourse, which included this old Chinese fable:

> A man travelling through the country came to a large city, very rich and splendid; he looked at it and said to his guide, "This must be a very righteous people, for I can only see but one little devil in this great city."
>
> The guide replied, "You do not understand, sir. This city is so perfectly given up to wickedness . . . that it requires but one devil to keep them all in subjection."
>
> Travelling on a little further, he came to a rugged path and saw an old man trying to get up the hill side, surrounded by seven great, big, coarse-looking devils.
>
> "Why," says the traveller, "this must be a tremendously wicked old man! Only see how many devils there are around him!"
>
> "This," replied the guide, "is the only righteous man in the country; and there are seven of the biggest devils trying to turn him out of his path, and they all cannot do it."
>
> After relating the fable, Elder Smith added that "the Devil has . . . the whole world . . . so perfectly at his disposal, that it only takes a very few devils to keep them all in subjection" and that "the whole legion of devils have nothing to do but look after the 'Mormons' and stir up the hearts of the children of men to destroy them — to put them out of existence." (*Journal of Discourses,* 5:363–64.)

Anti-Christs

The evil one has attempted on many occasions in all dispensations to put out of existence, if you will, many of

God's children. Sometimes he, himself, has assumed the deluder's role. Other times he has worked through those who have stepped to his side of the line. For instance, in the Book of Mormon, we read of three anti-Christs. Each was deceived, each preached against those who believed in Christ, and each sought openly to destroy the Church of God. Their patterns of deceit were similar. They taught false doctrines, spread lies, referred to prophecies as foolish traditions, accused Church leaders of perverting the right way of God, and baited the people by referring to their faith as a foolish and vain hope (see Jacob 7; Alma 1; and Alma 30).

When we read about the anti-Christs of former days, we marvel at how perverted their thinking became, and we marvel at how successful they were in their deceptions. We also wonder why some of the people were so gullible—so easily misled. And with all this marveling and wondering, we tend to put the anti-Christs in some corner of ancient history and go about our unguarded ways. This is dangerous. It could result in loss of faith; and, in a spiritual sense, it could put us out of existence.

Since the spring of 1820, Lucifer has led a relentless attack against the Latter-day Saints and their leaders. A parade of anti-Christs, anti-Mormons, and apostate groups have appeared on the scene. Many are still among us and have released new floods of lies and false accusations. These faith-killers and testimony-thieves use personal contacts, the printed word, electronic media, and other means of communication to sow doubts and disturb the peace of true believers.

Some time ago I received a tender letter from a bishop. He informed me that he had been involved in the excommunication of a recent convert. The new convert had fallen under the influence of a very dedicated apostate who was successful in destroying the convert's testimony. It seems that, to discredit Joseph Smith and subsequent prophets, the apostate cited changes made in Church publications over the years.

The approach used by the apostate is common among those who are more interested in shadows than in light. Their logic, if followed, would have them burning the New Testament because Luke's account of the gospel is not exactly like Matthew's or because the book of Acts reports two differing versions of Paul's vision on the road to Damascus (see Acts 9:1–9 and 22:4–11). Belief in modern prophets and continuous revelation is absent in the lives of many apostates. They would pin their hopes for salvation upon things other than those related to living prophets and living faith.

A Nine-Step Plan

How do we respond to such malicious and evil designs? Do we strike back? Allow me to suggest a course of action — one that is in harmony with the teachings of the Savior and that, if followed, will be in harmony with the wise counsel of prophets past and present:

1. *Avoid those who would tear down your faith.* Faith-killers are to be shunned. The seeds they plant in the mind and heart grow like cancer and eat away the Spirit. True messengers of God are builders — not destroyers. We send our missionaries into the world to teach and to help people receive truth line upon line until the fulness of the gospel is received (see D&C 98:12). As one new convert testified, "My previous church provided me the chapter on mortality. The Church of Jesus Christ of Latter-day Saints added two more chapters pertaining to the premortal and postmortal existences."

2. *Keep the commandments.* President Brigham Young promised, "All we have to do is to go onward and upward,

and keep the commandments of our Father and God; and he will confound our enemies" (*Discourses of Brigham Young*, sel. John A. Widtsoe [Salt Lake City: Deseret Book Company, 1957], p. 347). If we obey holy laws, we will take upon ourselves "the whole armour of God," and we will be able to stand against the wiles of the devil (see Ephesians 6:11–18). Moreover, obedience ensures us the guidance and protection of the Holy Spirit.

3. *Follow the living prophets.* President Heber J. Grant taught: "Always keep your eye on the President of the Church, and if he ever tells you to do anything, and it is wrong, and you do it, the Lord will bless you for it. . . . But you don't need to worry. The Lord will never let his mouthpiece lead the people astray" (quoted by Marion G. Romney in *Conference Report*, October 1960, p. 78). We walk in uncharted mine fields and place our souls in jeopardy when we receive the teachings of anyone except he that is ordained of God (see D&C 43:2–7; 52:9).

4. *Do not contend or debate over points of doctrine.* The Master warned "The spirit of contention is not of me, but is of the devil" (3 Nephi 11:29). We are inconsistent if we resort to Satanic tactics in attempting to achieve righteous ends. Such inconsistency results only in frustration, loss of the Spirit, and ultimate defeat. Remember, "we claim the privilege of worshiping Almighty God according to the dictates of our own conscience, and allow all men the same privilege" (Eleventh Article of Faith).

5. *Search the scriptures.* Few of us would go astray or lose our way if we regarded the scriptures as our personal guide or compass (see Alma 37:44). The iron rod is the word of God, and if we hold to it, we will not fall.

6. *Do not be swayed or diverted from the mission of the Church.* There are those who would draw you off course and cause you to waste time and energy. Satan used a di-

version ploy when he tempted Christ in the wilderness. The Savior's decisive response, "Get thee hence, Satan" (Matthew 4:10), is a proper example for all of us.

7. *Pray for your enemies.* Christ said to the Nephites, "Love your enemies, bless them that curse you, do good to them that hate you, and pray for them who despitefully use you and persecute you" (3 Nephi 12:44; see also Matthew 5:44; 3 Nephi 12:10–12). While on the cross, the Savior pleaded, "Father, forgive them; for they know not what they do" (Luke 23:34). Many people are kept from the truth — not because they don't want it, but because they know not where to find it (see D&C 123:12).

8. *Practice "pure religion."* Involve yourself in Christian service. Succor the needs of the sick and poor; visit the fatherless and widows, and be charitable to all, whether in the Church or out of the Church (see James 1:27 and Alma 1:30).

9. *Remember that there may be many questions for which we have no answers and that some things have to be accepted simply on faith.* An angel of the Lord asked Adam, "Why dost thou offer sacrifices unto the Lord?" He answered, "I know not, save the Lord commanded me" (Moses 5:6). There may be times when we are called upon to climb Mount Moriahs and to sacrifice our Isaacs without a full and prior explanation. Faith is the first principle of the gospel; it is a principle of progress.

I suggest that there are few who know better the reality of Satan and his accomplices than do those who faithfully serve the Lord, for they are exposed to the fiery darts of the adversary, which come whistling overhead as they labor in the front lines in our war against sin. However, I promise you and all who serve that if the nine actions above are followed consistently, victory will be yours and faith and testimony will be preserved.

Assurances

At the same time, I assure you that opposition to our cause testifies of its divinity. Would satanic powers combine against us if we were not posing a threat to such powers?

I assure you that there must be "opposition in all things," just as Lehi taught, to fulfill the purpose of mortality and to draw from us the finest effort (see 2 Nephi 2:11). One writer penned this profound thought:

> A ship, like a human being, moves best when it is slightly athwart the wind, when it has to keep its sails tight and attend its course. Ships, like men, do poorly when the wind is directly behind, pushing them sloppily on their way so that no care is required in steering or in the management of sails; the wind seems favorable, for it blows in the direction one is heading, but actually it is destructive because it induces a relaxation in tension and skill. What is needed is a wind slightly opposed to the ship, for then tension can be maintained, and juices can flow and ideas can germinate, for ships, like men, respond to challenge. (James A. Michener, *Chesapeake* [New York: Random House, 1978], p. 566; see also D&C 123:16.)

I assure you that opposition, if met and overcome, has a refining influence upon our lives. A verse in one of our hymns reads:

> *When through fiery trials thy pathway shall lie,*
> *My grace, all sufficient, shall be thy supply.*
> *The flame shall not hurt thee; I only design*
> *Thy dross to consume and thy gold to refine.*
> ("How Firm a Foundation," *Hymns*, no. 85.)

The Savior learned obedience by the things he suffered (see Hebrews 5:8). Joseph Smith's oppositions gave him experience and worked for his good (see D&C 122:7).

I assure you that the waters in which we are wont to

swim are but little puddles when compared with the deep rivers of opposition in which the Prophet Joseph and others swam (see D&C 127:2).

I assure you that our cause is just and that it will succeed, regardless of the opposition exerted against us. Earlier Saints were bolstered by these words: "As well might man stretch forth his puny arm to stop the Missouri river in its decreed course, or to turn it up stream, as to hinder the Almighty from pouring down knowledge from heaven upon the heads of the Latter-day Saints" (D&C 121:33).

President Brigham Young said: "Every time you kick 'Mormonism' you kick it upstairs; you never kick it downstairs. The Lord Almighty so orders it" (*Discourses of Brigham Young*, p. 351).

An Appeal

With all my heart I implore you to walk not on the fringes of our faith but to seek the safety of the center. This can be done best by counseling with your leaders, observing Church guidelines, receiving nourishment from the good word of God, and remaining within the fellowshipping circle of the Saints.

Do not permit faithless people to turn you out of the right way or to put you out of existence (see Moroni 6). Guard against discouragement. Keep your mind riveted upon the sacred calling you have received.

I do pray for those who deal in the highest form of larceny—that of stripping people of their precious testimonies. Such action, if continued, will lead only to the futility and emptiness of the dream of a night vision (see 2 Nephi 27:3; Acts 5:33–39).

May God help you and all of us in our war against sin. Though our numbers may be few and our dominions small, may we go forward with confidence and "armed with righ-

teousness and with the power of God in great glory" (1
Nephi 14:14).

Find refuge and reassurance against opposition by med-
itating often upon these words of the Savior:

> Blessed are all they who are persecuted for my name's
> sake, for theirs is the kingdom of heaven.
>
> And blessed are ye when men shall revile you and
> persecute, and shall say all manner of evil against you
> falsely, for my sake; for ye shall have great joy and be
> exceedingly glad, for great shall be your reward in heaven;
> for so persecuted they the prophets who were before you.
> (3 Nephi 12:10–12.)

Chapter Sixteen

Knowing and Living the Law of Sacrifice

Once in our sacrament service, a young man who would be entering the Missionary Training Center in Provo in a few days was one of the main speakers. The prospective missionary did very well.

However, he made a point of the fact that he was sacrificing many things in order to serve a full-time mission. He mentioned that he was giving up or postponing his education, marriage, and other precious plans for the future.

I do not fault anything the missionary said. He was obviously sincere in expressing himself the way he did. But, I do wonder whether the young man really understood the law of sacrifice and its true relationship to serving the Lord. I also wonder whether you might be interested in learning more about this important principle of the gospel as it relates to magnifying a calling in the Church.

Personal Sacrifice

Many years ago, I delayed my formal education, gave up a promising sports career, and interrupted my marriage to serve a full-time mission for the Church. At the time I felt that I was placing my all upon the altar of God, making a significant personal sacrifice. Some well-meaning people added to my feelings of self-pity by saying I was giving away my future; others said I was forfeiting the best years of my life. Yes, I was led to presume that by serving the mission, I would place the Lord deeply in my debt.

How very wrong I was! Even before my mission ended, the blessings came flowing upon me. And, that stream of goodness from heaven has continued over the years and seems to be never ending. What little I gave to the Lord has been returned to me in "good measure, pressed down, and shaken together, and running over" (Luke 6:38). No, the mission was not a sacrifice; it was a simple test of my faith and a time for God to verify his promise, which is, "Seek not the things of this world, but seek ye first to build up the Kingdom of God, and to establish his righteousness; . . . and all these things shall be added unto you" (JST Matthew 6:38).

Sacrifice—The Crowning Test

Sacrifice has been referred to as the crowning test of the gospel. Joseph Smith taught, "A religion that does not require the sacrifice of all things never has power sufficient to produce the faith necessary [to lead] unto life and salvation" (*Lectures on Faith* [Salt Lake City: Deseret Book Company, 1985], 6:7).

In response to the rich young man's query about how to obtain eternal life, the Savior answered that he must be willing to sacrifice all that he had for the Lord and his cause. Said Jesus, "If thou wilt be perfect, go and sell that thou hast, and give to the poor, and thou shalt have treasure in heaven: and come and follow me" (see Matthew 19:16–29; D&C 132:55).

Modern-day Sacrifices

How does the principle and practice of sacrifice apply in a modern world? What sacrifices are we required to make in this the twentieth century? What do we place upon God's altar?

President Spencer W. Kimball stated:

> We must lay on the altar and sacrifice whatever is required by the Lord. We begin by [1] offering a "broken heart and a contrite spirit." We follow this by [2] giving our best effort in our assigned fields of labor and callings. We learn our duty and execute it fully. Finally we [3] consecrate our time, talents, and means as called upon by our file leaders and as prompted by the whisperings of the Spirit. . . . And as we give, we find that "sacrifice brings forth the blessings of heaven!" [*Hymns*, no. 147.] And in the end, we learn it was no sacrifice at all. (*Conference Report*, April 1978, pp. 123–24.)

Let me comment about the three offerings cited by President Kimball:

1. *A broken heart and contrite spirit.* Words used to define a broken heart and contrite spirit include *humility, meekness, penitence, remorse,* and *repentance.* Those whose hearts are broken and whose spirits are contrite are teachable, submissive to the will of God, and anxious to forsake all forms of evil. Such people are willing to give away all their sins, have no more disposition to do wrong, and are obedient to holy commandments (see Alma 22:15–18; Mosiah 5:1–3). Note this meaningful scripture: "Verily I say unto you, all among them who know their hearts are honest, and are broken, and their spirits contrite, and are

willing to observe their covenants by sacrifice—yea, every sacrifice which I, the Lord, shall command—they are accepted of me" (D&C 97:8).

2. *Giving our best effort.* All Church workers have the responsibility to learn their duties and to act accordingly (see D&C 107:99–100). They must not wait to be commanded or compelled into action; they must "be anxiously engaged in a good cause, and do many things of their own free will, and bring to pass much righteousness" (D&C 58:26–28).

If we labor in our callings as faithfully as did Jacob, the brother of Nephi, perhaps we, too, might declare, "We did magnify our office unto the Lord, taking upon us the responsibility, answering the sins of the people upon our own heads if we did not teach them the word of God with all diligence. . . . [we] did magnify [our] office with soberness" (Jacob 1:19; 2:2).

If we can make that declaration in all honesty, we will have placed upon the altar of God an acceptable offering.

3. *Consecrate time, talents, and means.* I view a calling as an ideal time to learn and to practice living the law of consecration, for it allows us to consecrate our time, talents, and means as acceptable offerings to God. Of course, our consecration of self and means is to be done in harmony with the requirements and expectations received from file or priesthood leaders and from the Holy Spirit.

I especially like what President Kimball said about sacrificing in accord with the "whisperings of the Spirit." Such truth has been proven in my own life and can be illustrated with a personal experience.

A bishop came to our home and invited us to contribute to the Jordan River Temple fund. We had never before enjoyed the privilege of making this kind of contribution, and we were eager to do so. I said to the bishop, "How much do you want us to give?" He quoted an amount, thanked us, and left our home. Once he was gone, my wife turned to me and said, "The amount of money suggested by the bishop is but a pittance; I feel that we can and should give more." I had similar feelings, for the Spirit within was speaking loud and clear.

We did, therefore, give an amount beyond that expected by our file leader, as prompted by the whisperings of the Spirit. Consequently, we were blessed abundantly and gained that peace of conscience that is synonymous with joy.

God tested Abraham by asking him to place his son Isaac upon the altar. God tests us by asking us to place our time, talents, and resources upon that same altar. If we yield our will to the Lord's will, as did Abraham and Isaac, not withholding anything from God, we shall be blessed and prospered in many ways (see Genesis 22:12, 16). But, if we pay tithing grudgingly, serve stintingly, or withhold our offering to any degree, we shall lose the full blessings associated with the law of sacrifice.

Jonah was called to serve the Lord by calling the people of Nineveh to repentance. He attempted to withhold from the Lord, to ignore the call, and to follow his own selfish desires. He reaped the bitter consequences of his decision and fell on bad times. Later, however, he repented and declared to the Lord: "I will sacrifice unto thee with the voice of thanksgiving; I will pay that that I have vowed. Salvation is of the Lord" (Jonah 2:9).

So it is with all of us. We, too, have made sacred vows, including the vow to live the law of sacrifice. Are we fulfilling our vows? Are we making acceptable sacrifices through the payment of tithes and offerings and Church service? Are we in process of passing the crowning test of the gospel?

A Lesson in Liberality

I have always found inspiration in the allegorical account of a meeting of our Lord and a beggar as told by the famous Indian poet and composer, Sir Rabindranath Tagore. The writer represents the beggar as speaking:

> I had been begging from door to door along the country road, when thy golden chariot appeared in the distance, like a glittering dream, and I wondered who this King of Kings might be.
>
> My expectations grew and I thought that my days of hardship now had come to an end. I stood there expecting that alms would be given without solicitation, and that gold would be strewn abroad in all directions in the sand.
>
> The chariot stopped where I stood. Thy eyes saw me when Thou didst descend smiling. I felt that the fortune of my life had come. Suddenly, Thou didst stretch forth Thy right hand and didst say: "What hast thou to give me?"
>
> What a royal joke: To show the empty hand of a beggar!
>
> I was confused. I stood there hesitating. Slowly I took from my scrip the smallest grain of corn and gave it to Thee. But great was my astonishment, when, in the evening, I emptied the scrip on the floor and found a very small grain of gold in the miserable pile.
>
> Then I wept bitterly and wished that I had had it in my heart to give Thee all!

This parable requires little comment. To those in the Lord's service, the lesson is very plain. What we give to the Master does turn to gold in our own satchels or lives, and we can never put the Lord in our debt (see Mosiah 2:20–24).

Bitter Tears

I supervised a missionary who served grudgingly for twenty-two months. During that time, he enjoyed little or no success, offended several companions, and never felt the spirit of his calling. He threatened to quit many times. Often, I felt inclined to honor his threats. Still, I felt within my heart that he had something to offer and that he could succeed, if only he experienced a change of heart.

The young man and I discussed his situation thoroughly and concurred that he had been serving his way and not the Lord's way. He acknowledged that he had placed little or nothing upon the altar. After a long conversation, he agreed to live and work for one month in accord with mission rules and programs. I agreed to provide him with an excellent companion and to place him in a productive area. We both agreed that he would call me at the end of the month and tell me whether he wanted to stay and finish his mission.

I received and read his weekly reports eagerly. They were startling! He and his companion were teaching many lessons and converting several people. In fact, by the end of that "special agreement" month, he had participated in more gospel discussions and convert baptisms than the rest of his mission combined.

At the close of the month he failed to call me, so I called him. I asked why he had not contacted me as we had agreed. He explained that he had been too busy to call. He closed the telephone conversation by saying, "Leave me here forever; I'm having a ball!"

Another month passed, and the missionary was slated to return home. He came to the mission home for his final interview and a farewell testimonial. None of us could believe our eyes. The change in the young man's spirit and demeanor was startling. His apathy had been replaced by enthusiasm, his glumness had been dispelled by a radiant smile, and his negative attitude had been pushed aside by an optimistic spirit.

I shall never forget the testimony he bore. He acknowledged that he had wasted the majority of his time in the mission field. His words were, "I have only served a two-month mission." And, like the beggar in Tagore's allegory, the young man wept bitterly because he had not had it in his heart to give the Lord his all.

Privilege or Sacrifice?

In 1853, President Brigham Young declared:

> I hear people talk about their troubles, their sore privations, and the great sacrifices they have made for the Gospel's sake. It never was a sacrifice to me. Anything I can do or suffer in the cause of the Gospel, is only like dropping a pin into the sea; the blessings, gifts, powers, honour, joy, truth, salvation, glory, immortality, and eternal lives, as far outswell anything I can do in return for such precious gifts, as the great ocean exceeds in expansion, bulk, and weight, the pin that I drop into it. . . . Suppose I should be called to preach the Gospel until my head is white, and my limbs become weak with age, until I go down into my grave, and never see my family and friends again in the flesh, would it be a sacrifice? No, but one of the greatest blessings that could be conferred upon mortal man, to have the privilege of calling thousands, and perhaps millions, from darkness to light, from the power of Satan and unrighteousness to the principles of truth and righteousness in the living God. (*Journal of Discourses*, 1:313–14.)

To President Young, missionary service was a privilege, not a sacrifice. Such was the case because he had an eternal perspective of things. He was not hindered by the sometimes narrow view of impatient youth; he viewed things through mature eyes and could see beyond tomorrow and the next day. He knew that life was quick in passing and that some things have eternal value and eternal consequences.

Conclusion

God help us to climb our personal mountains of Moriah and to place our all upon the altar of God. In so doing, we shall be blessed beyond measure and demonstrate our devotion to a loving Father in Heaven and his Son, the "great and last sacrifice" (Alma 34:14), in whose debt we shall stand eternally.

"Like unto Angels of God"

In a revelation specified as "embracing the law of the Church," the elders at Kirtland, Ohio, were commanded to preach the gospel in a certain manner. Among other things, they were informed that they should be properly ordained, teach the principles of the gospel found in the Bible and the Book of Mormon, receive the Spirit through the prayer of faith, and build up the Church in every region. But, of all the instructions given in this inspired scripture, none was more illuminating than the injunction that they were to declare the Lord's word "like unto angels of God" (D&C 42, section heading and verse 6).

The Savior used the words "like unto" time and time again as he taught in parables. For example, he said that the kingdom of heaven was "like unto a certain king" (Matthew 22:2); "like unto a treasure" (Matthew 13:44); "like unto a merchant man" (Matthew 13:45); "like unto a net" (Matthew 13:47); and "like unto a man that is an householder" (Matthew 20:1). In each of these instances and more, the analogies drawn by the Master Teacher were vivid and full of hidden meaning to the true believer. Each comparison made between the kingdom of heaven and a person or thing painted a picture in the mind of the listener; yet, each comparison served merely as a working sketch to those who pondered Christ's words and who wanted to brush in further detail or add deeper color.

Angelic Commissions

The detail and color of the expression "like unto angels" begins with the prophet Mormon's instructions concerning the office and calling of angels. Mormon recorded that angels are subject to God and "minister according to the word of his command, showing themselves unto them of strong faith and a firm mind in every form of godliness" (Moroni 7:30). He also stated that the office of an angel's ministry is "[1] to call men unto repentance, and [2] to fulfil and to do the work of the covenants of the Father, which he hath made unto the children of men, [3] to prepare the way among the children of men, by declaring the word of Christ unto the chosen vessels of the Lord, that they may bear testimony of him" (Moroni 7:31).

We can readily see that the office and calling of angels is similar to other offices and callings commissioned by the Lord, for nearly any Church service includes crying repentance, fulfilling covenants, preparing the way of the Lord, declaring the word of Christ, and ministering according to God's commands. Hence, we can conclude that those who are called to Church service are given angelic commissions; their office and calling is like unto that of angels.

The Tongue of Angels

Nephi spoke of the power of the tongue or language of angels, which anyone in Church service should learn to use.

Said he: "Do ye not remember that I said unto you that after ye had received the Holy Ghost ye could speak with the tongue of angels? And now, how could ye speak with the tongue of angels save it were by the Holy Ghost? Angels speak by the power of the Holy Ghost; wherefore, they speak the words of Christ. Wherefore, I said unto you, feast upon the words of Christ; for behold, the words of Christ will tell you all things what ye should do" (2 Nephi 32:2–3).

Of all the best gifts, perhaps none is to be sought more earnestly than the ability to speak with the tongue of angels. Success in many callings depends in large measure upon the convincing power of voice and word. Without the tongue of angels, the servants of God are just ordinary men and women; but, armed with the Spirit and the words of Christ, they become "like unto angels" and teach persuasively and powerfully.

The Faces of Angels

I was told of an incident where two missionaries were stopped by a woman on a city walkway. The woman asked, "Who are you?" Before they could answer, she added, "You look like angels."

This story does not sound farfetched to those who are acquainted with the sanctifying influence of service and who have observed the special look of those who are close to the Spirit of the Lord. There is a glow and aura that seem to surround those who walk uprightly before the Lord, seeking to advance his cause of righteousness.

We are reminded of the scriptural account where the faces of two brothers, Nephi and Lehi, were seen through a cloud of darkness. The record notes, "They did shine exceedingly, even as the faces of angels" (Helaman 5:36).

Those called to the Lord's work are expected to undergo a spiritual rebirth and to receive God's image in their countenances (see Alma 5:14). Such will occur as they experience a change of heart, exercise faith, keep themselves unspotted from the sins of the world, and seek to serve "like unto angels of God" (see Alma 5:13–19).

Treated like Angels

Few scriptural accounts are more inspiring than the experiences of Ammon and the sons of Mosiah, as recorded in the Book of Mormon. They not only served faithfully but did so for a long period among a wicked and perverse people. In due time, however, they won the hearts of the Lamanites, converted many, and eventually referred to their former enemies as their "dearly beloved." This love was apparently reciprocated by the Lamanites, for we read, "They [Ammon and his associates] were treated as though they were angels sent from God to save them from everlasting destruction" (Alma 27:4).

On occasion, the faithful servants of God are mistreated. Generally, however, they are loved and held in high esteem — even like unto angels — by the people they serve. For example, Church members generally shower their love upon the missionaries who serve among them, and some converts almost worship the missionaries who were instrumental in bringing them the gospel and its saving ordinances.

Conclusion

Other scriptural references could be cited and discussed relating to angels and those called to Church service. The list is long and colorful, since the two groups have a common commission and mutual interests. And, it would be well to study this subject in greater detail. Suffice it to say that we are expected to live, speak, and serve in an angelic fashion. We must "arouse the faculties of [our] souls" and become men and women of Christ, else we will fall short of our sacred and holy commissions (see Jacob 3:11).

With all my heart I pray that the contents of this book will enable you and others to do the Lord's work "like unto angels of God." At the same time, I hope that the advice given will stir a desire within the hearts of more than a few to feel as Alma felt when he cried: "O that I were an angel, and could have the wish of mine heart, that I might go forth and speak with the trump of God, with a voice to shake the earth, and cry repentance unto every people! Yea, I would declare unto every soul, as with the voice of thunder, repentance and the plan of redemption, that they should repent and come unto our God, that there might not be more sorrow upon all the face of the earth" (Alma 29:1–2).

May God bless you and all others who have been called to the Lord's work to serve the Lord and your fellowmen properly. May you retain in your heart this wonderful promise: "Whoso receiveth you, there I will be also, for I will go before your face. I will be on your right hand and on your left, and my Spirit shall be in your hearts, and mine angels round about you, to bear you up" (D&C 84:88).

Index